WHITTLING

A Step-by-Step Guide to Wood Carving and Fun Whittling Projects for Beginners

By Tony Gordon

WHITTLING

© **Copyright 2020 - All rights reserved.**

The content contained within this book may not be reproduced, duplicated or transmitted without direct written permission from the author or the publisher.

Under no circumstances will any blame or legal responsibility be held against the publisher, or author, for any damages, reparation, or monetary loss due to the information contained within this book. Either directly or indirectly.

<u>Legal Notice:</u>

This book is copyright protected. This book is only for personal use. You cannot amend, distribute, sell, use, quote or paraphrase any part, or the content within this book, without the consent of the author or publisher.

<u>Disclaimer Notice:</u>

Please note the information contained within this document is for educational and entertainment purposes only. All effort has been executed to present accurate, up to date, and reliable, complete information. No warranties of any kind are declared or implied. Readers acknowledge that the author is not engaging in the rendering of legal, financial, medical or professional advice. The content within this book has been derived from various sources. Please consult a licensed professional before attempting any techniques outlined

WHITTLING

in this book.

By reading this document, the reader agrees that under no circumstances is the author responsible for any losses, direct or indirect, which are incurred as a result of the use of information contained within this document, including, but not limited to, — errors, omissions, or inaccuracies.

WHITTLING

Table of Contents

Introduction vii

Chapter One: Getting Started 1

Choosing the Right Knife 2

Choosing the Wood 6

Keeping Your Knife Sharp 9

Understanding Wood Grain 13

Safety Precautions 16

Chapter Two: Whittling Cutting Techniques 22

The Straightaway Rough Cut 23

The Pull Cut 24

The Push Cut 25

The V-Cut 26

The Stop Cut 28

Step-by-Step: The Straightaway Rough Cut 29

Step-by-Step: The Pull Cut 30

Step-by-Step: The Push Cut 31

Step-by-Step: The V-Cut 32

Step-by-Step: The Stop Cut 33

WHITTLING

Chapter Three: Common Mistakes to Avoid Before You Start 37

Only Work With Good Lighting 39

Never Whittle With a Dull Knife 40

Choose the Right Wood 41

Don't Whittle While Tired 42

Chapter Four: Fun Projects for Beginners 45

Animal Animations 49

Flights of Fancy 51

Games Galore 55

Holiday Hobbies 59

Home and Garden Décor 64

Lettered Messages 68

Natural Designs 72

Painted Projects 77

Survival Skills 82

Art for Art's Sake 87

Chapter Five: Advanced Projects 92

Animal Animations 93

Flights of Fancy 96

Games Galore 100

WHITTLING

Holiday Hobbies 103

Home and Garden Décor 108

Interlocking Leisures 113

Natural Designs 116

Painted Projects 121

Survival Skills 125

Some Big Ideas 129

Final Words **135**

WHITTLING

INTRODUCTION

Crafting is one of the most fulfilling activities a person can do with their time. To make something unique out of raw materials is among the highest achievements that we humans have conquered. We've turned fur into blankets, pillows and sweaters. We've turned metal into vehicles, sculptures and furniture. We've taken wood and turned it into tables, chairs, walkways and even buildings. Hundreds of thousands of people are drawn to create, to transform the ideas in their minds into real, tactile creations that improve the lives of those around them. Crafting, indeed, is a beautiful thing.

However, certain crafting endeavors can be expensive and take time and effort to undertake. Take a look at woodworking, as just one example. You need a space where you can work the wood, large enough for the projects but also with ventilation to prevent damage to the lungs. You will need a handful of tools at the minimum, but even a fairly modest collection can cost you several hundred dollars – especially if you invest in machine tools. Plus, you need to learn how to use each of them and how to join wood together with end joints, screws, nails and glue. It's easy to see where all that money, time and effort disappear in a highly technical craft such as woodworking.

But woodworking isn't the only way to work with wood to create amazing and beautiful pieces of art. In fact, one of the cheapest and easiest forms of crafting is done with wood: whittling. Whittling only requires two pieces of equipment. Although, you can invest in some additional tools should you become more advanced. But, to begin, you only need a knife to whittle the wood and the wood you want to whittle. Pretty simple.

Whittling is also known as wood carving because that's essentially what it is. You use a knife to carve into a piece of wood. If it sounds simple, that's because it is. But don't confuse the simplicity of the act as a sign of its unimportance or of its limitations. You can make thousands upon thousands of amazing creations by whittling away at wood. Consider all of the amazing sculptures in museums all over the world. While many of most well-preserved artifacts are made of stone – because stone outlasts wood, which is more prone to rot and decay – these same artifacts could be made of wood: sculpting is merely an advanced form of whittling. In fact, it is likely that many of the stone and marble monuments that we see in museums were originally conceived of and carved of wood. Wood is, quite simply, more readily available and easier to work with than stone materials, not to mention that the tools needed to carve wood are simpler. Many of the projects we look at in this book will be on the simpler side of things, though we will be moving into advanced territory by the end, but you could conceivably make Michelangelo's *David* with a large enough piece of wood – and a fair amount of patience.

Considering how much control whittling can give you to make your artworks and creations, it truly is amazing that all you need is a knife and some wood. You could work on your project from the comfort of your living room chair, around the fire on a camping trip, or even while sitting in the car waiting to pick up your children from school. You can whittle anywhere that you can legally brandish a knife. Unfortunately, this means that the airport and some bustling public places are out of contention, but pretty much everything else is open.

In this book, you'll learn all about whittling or wood carving. Chapter one will walk you through picking the right knife and the right wood for your projects. We'll cover safety precautions, how to keep your knife sharp, and what you need to understand about wood grain. This covers the equipment you need to get started and how to understand and look after it for longevity's sake.

Chapter two will move into whittling techniques. The different techniques such as the pull stroke, push stroke, and straight rough cut will be covered. But it isn't enough simply to tell you about them. We'll walk through them step-by-step so you can be assured of your

WHITTLING

ability to follow along. Chapter three will take a look at the mistakes beginners commonly make, providing you with information to avoid these mistakes. With awareness, you'll be able to keep an eye out to ensure you don't fall into the same traps that many beginners before you have.

We'll then close out the book with chapters four and five. These are the real meat of this volume. Chapter four will introduce you to projects that are a lot of fun for beginners. These are easier carvings for you to practice your whittling skills. They'll have challenges of their own for you to overcome, but for the most part, they will be short and sweet; that way you can quickly finish your first few projects to get a taste of the sense of pride that comes with completion. Chapter five will look at more advanced projects, the kind of projects which require more time and attention to get right. Projects in chapter five will be longer than those in chapter four and you'll likely find that you need to work on them over many sessions in order to complete them.

By the end of this book, you'll have learned how to pick a whittling knife, select the right wood, and employ all the techniques you need to carve your own amazing projects. Soon you will be producing small masterpieces of your own. Don't wait: let's whittle!

CHAPTER ONE

GETTING STARTED

Getting started with whittling is incredibly easy. Truly there isn't another craft that requires so little. Even painting or drawing takes more than whittling since you'll typically use multiple colors or pencil sizes. All you need to whittle is some wood and a knife.

But there is a little more to it than that, of course. Not every knife is made the same and not every type of wood performs identically. Then there's the need to understand wood grain since it has a direct connection to the final product you're creating. There's also the need to keep yourself safe and to ensure that your knife is in the best working condition possible. So, while it is simple to get started whittling, a few points must be covered first.

In this chapter, we'll start by picking out the right knife and move on to a look at different types of wood so we can ensure we select the best wood for the job at hand. After that, we'll cover understanding wood grain, keeping our knife sharp and then finish out the chapter with those safety precautions we mentioned. Let's dive right in. The faster we do the sooner we can get carving!

Choosing the Right Knife

For our first section in the book, we start with understanding how to choose the right knife. But not just any knife.

Oh wait, we are just starting with any knife. You can technically whittle wood with any knife you have available to you. It is truly that easy of a hobby to pick up. If you don't have money to purchase a knife for whittling then you can absolutely make do with what you have available to you. While you could use a large kitchen knife, you'll find that a larger knife doesn't offer the level of control you'll want. Use a smaller knife instead, something the size of a steak knife should be the upper limit and even at this size, the knife is going to be a little unwieldy.

If you are willing to spend a little money then there are some specialty whittling knives available on the market. A specialty whittling knife will have a fixed blade to ensure a firm cut with each stroke. You will also find that most of the specialty whittling knives on the market come with a comfortable grip, often curved, so it fits

WHITTLING

naturally in the recess of the hand. One such knife that has been specially made for wood carving is the Morakniv Wood Carving 120. Another from Morakniv is their Wood Carving 164 that has a hooked blade to help with detailing. In fact, Morakniv is pretty much the top of the line for wood carving blades; although, Flexcut is another company that produce great blades. You could actually purchase quite a few blades through these companies, each designed for specific wood carving techniques or situations. This could get expensive pretty quickly and the beginner is best leaving these alone until they are comfortable with wood carving and know they want to keep up the hobby.

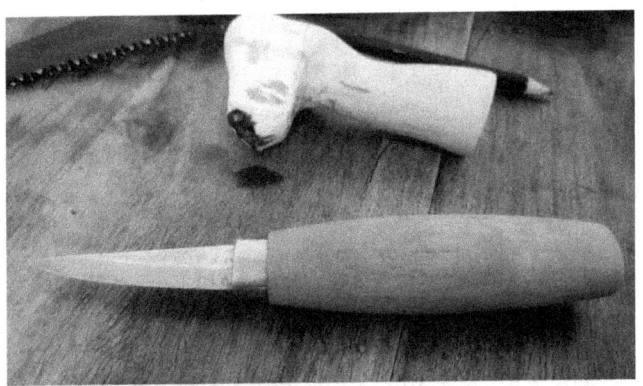

The best bet for the beginner is to get a pocket knife. Many of you reading this book already have one lying around the house. You might not use it for much but they're one of the tools that seem to proliferate in households all over the world. They have a thousand and one uses and you wouldn't want to go camping without one. You also wouldn't want to whittle without one, according to tons of top-tier woodcarvers. Wood carving has a history tied closely to that of the pocket knife. Much like how many people consider boar hair the only fibre to use with a beard brush, many consider pocket knives the only way to whittle wood. They're typically inexpensive. They're easy to carry around and they tend to have multiple styles of blade collected in one tool. Now, they're not going to offer as much strength as a fixed blade would but that just means you need to learn to support the blade from behind with a stiff finger as you cut.

So, if you're looking for the right knife to start whittling, then you can't go wrong with a pocket knife. Failing that, you can use pretty much any knife you have available but you just need to understand that you are giving up a measure of control the larger the knife is. If you take a liking to whittling, then there are plenty of specialty knives you can purchase and collect. But I suggest starting small and getting a feel for wood carving before you invest too heavily into it.

There are also numerous wood carving tool kits and sets that can help a beginner get started with particular projects: for example, a spoon carving kit comes with a hook knife to help you with rounded cuts, such as for making wooden spoons and bowls by hand. In addition to a hook knife, you can also invest in a chip knife which is used for cutting out the smallest details. Some

WHITTLING

dedicated hobbyists also recommend a gouge knife for help in relief carving. There are also wood carving sets that come with various blades of various sizes so that you can engage in intricate designs or detailed work; these can be pricey, however, so you should be sure that you want to invest the time in the hobby before you invest too much money.

WHITTLING

Choosing the Wood

Choosing the right wood for a particular project is a little bit more involved than choosing the right knife. This is due to the simple fact that there are more options at your disposal for wood than there are with knives. With knives you have speciality blades, pocket knives and everything else. That gives us three options for knives. With wood, there are five main options.

Balsa: Balsa wood is a softwood, which means it will be quite easy to whittle into and, therefore, a great pick for beginners. Making it an even better option for beginners is its price. Balsa wood is quite inexpensive, which makes it easy to get your hands on plenty of it for your projects. If you're looking to practice, then balsa is a great pick; although, it isn't the most inexpensive option we'll look at. But if you want a little more sense of professionalism to your pieces rather than rustic charm, then it's the way beginners will want to go.

Basswood: Basswood is closely tied to the history of woodcarving, just as the pocket knife is closely tied to the history of whittling. Basswood was *the* wood of choice for the famous German sculptors of the Middle Ages. Not that there's any surprise there. After all, basswood has an incredibly soft texture. If you are working on designs that you need to trace or cut elaborate lines into, then it is pretty much perfect for it. It also doesn't have very much of a grain to it and this can be ideal for your projects. It'll cost you more than balsa wood does but it should be just as easy to find at your local art supplies store.

Pine: As we move into pine, we have a chance to explore some of the downsides of wood in terms of whittling. Pine is available pretty much all over the northern hemisphere and so it is even easier to find than balsa or basswood. The fact that it is so populous means that it is a rather inexpensive wood and you shouldn't have any issues finding it. But this only introduces us to the problem of freshness. Pine that has been dried out has issues with holding onto details when compared to our other types of wood thus explored. The grain tends to cause issues when cutting into dried pine. Then you might think the answer is to use fresh pine. You'd be on the right track since fresh pine certainly retains more detail when it comes to whittling but you'll find that the process of whittling is much slower with fresh pine because you need constantly to stop to clean pine sap off of your blade and the wood. This can make pine a frustrating wood to use; although, there are whittlers who absolutely love the stuff.

Random Twigs: The cheapest way to get into whittling is to start with the twigs and branches you find in your backyard or along any forest path. If you want to get down to it, then whittling on the random twigs and branches you find is most likely the truest and oldest form of whittling there is. It harkens back to sitting around the campfire with a stick you found in the nearby woods and wasting away the afternoon while you wait for the meat from the hunt to finish cooking. There is something primitive about using whatever wood you find and I mean that in a positive sense. I find that there is more of a sense of accomplishment from whittling a twig or piece of found wood than there is from whittling a block of specifically sized wood. However, there are many limitations to this form as the size of the project is determined by what wood you can find, so you can't perfectly plan out a project ahead of time to the same degree as you can with store-bought woods.

Everything Else: These are just the woods that are most effective when it comes to whittling. They have long histories of being used in the artform and this is directly related to how well they hold their shape or designs, as well as how easy they are to work with. But you can use just about any type of wood you can get your hands on. Harder woods will prove to be much more difficult than woods that are soft but this doesn't mean you can't achieve some amazing results. It just means that you are likely to find the experience much more frustrating and challenging than if you selected one of the above-listed woods. I certainly recommend using balsa wood or basswood if you have the choice but don't limit yourself to these if you can get started faster using some scraps you've got around the house. I find it is best to get started, even on a harder wood, than it is to put off starting until a later date. The more experience you can gain, the better you'll get. It's that simple. Start with what you can, rather than wait for what is ideal.

Keeping Your Knife Sharp

As you whittle away at your selected wood, you'll find that your knife dulls over time. This happens to the best of knives. Even if the only thing you were cutting was vegetables, eventually your knife would dull. Most of us aren't professional chefs so many of us don't worry about sharpening our kitchen knives. But if we want to be skilled whittlers, then we need to know how to sharpen our knives so that we make the best cuts we possibly can. Our cuts will improve the more we practice them but all the practice in the world can't make up for the sloppiness of a dull knife.

There are tons of ways you can sharpen a knife and we could go through all of them but is there really a point? So, as long as you can sharpen your knife, you can keep whittling. We'll look at one of the easier ways to sharpen a knife and use that for the time being. But this is one area in which you can learn, grow and develop based on what interests you the most and what techniques speak to you. For the time being, however, we're going to use a sharpening stone and some lubricant.

WHITTLING

There are many different sharpening stones for sale. From Japanese water stones to classic whetstones. You can even find stones covered with diamonds for sharpening if you want to get super fancy. But what's the point of dropping a ton of money right off the bat? For our purposes, all we need is a sharpening stone. Go into any hardware store, or even just do a quick Amazon search, and you'll have no problem finding a simple sharpening stone for a reasonable price. You shouldn't have to spend more than ten bucks on a stone and even that could be seen as pushing it. As for lubrication, we want to select a lubricant so that there is less heat generated when sharpening. As you sharpen, you create friction. This friction is what is doing the actual sharpening. But this friction generates heat and too much heat can actually lead to the molecules of the knife warping. This isn't a major issue if your blade isn't used for much but whereas we're using our blade for intricate details, we want to ensure that our blade is in the best possible condition. A lubricant such as mineral oil is a must. But you can find oil for knife sharpening in pretty much every hardware store and it should cost you even less than your sharpening stone.

Start by determining how dull the blade is. If it is pretty sharp but just starting to lose its edge, then you'll want to use the finer side of your sharpening stone. If it has lost quite a bit of its edge, then you'll start out with the rougher side of the sharpening stone. If you've ever worked with sandpaper, then you'll have an idea of how a lower grit count results in a rougher sanding. Sharpening stones are almost always rougher on one side than the other so that you can work a dull blade with a low grit count and prepare it for the higher grit count sharpening. Once you have determined which side you need to use, start the sharpening process by first applying lubricant over the appropriate side of the stone. You'll want to use plenty of oil but you don't need to soak the stone, just ensure that there's enough to cover the surface.

Sharpening your blade is as simple as running the blade over the stone again and again. But the tricky part is that you need to keep the angle the same each time. With a pocket knife, the type that most beginners are starting their whittling journey with, you'll want about a fifteen-degree angle. You can get this by first pressing the flat of the blade against the stone and then lifting it up to the proper angle. The hardest part of this whole process is keeping the angle the same. You can purchase a sharpening guide to help with this task but I've never found one that I particularly recommend. I find that this skill is easiest to practice until you've got it down. Once you have the technique, you can sharpen your knives no matter where you are without having to worry about whether or not you've got your sharpening guide handy.

How you sharpen your blade is up to you. Do you want to move the sharpening stone over the blade or do you want to move the blade over the sharpening stone?

WHITTLING

Do you want to stroke forward across the sharpening stone or backwards over it? It really doesn't matter which you use. The important thing here is that you find the movement that is most comfortable for you as well as which is the easiest to maintain a consistent sharpening angle. You want to apply a bit of pressure but you shouldn't be trying to push the blade through the stone. We're not looking to cut it, just to run over its surface with a bit of pressure. You should only need to do about ten passes with the sharpening stone per side. Once you finish sharpening one side it is important that you do the same thing to the other side. That means if you do ten strokes on one side, you do ten on the other. If you only did a quick six then the other side gets a quick six. We want to keep the blade as uniform as possible.

At this point some people like to alternate back and forth between the two sides, one stroke to the left then one to right. I personally don't worry about this step and I've never had a problem with my knife blades. But if you feel like yours isn't quite sharp enough then this can be done to fine-tune the sharpening just a bit.

If you started sharpening on the fine grit side of the stone, you're done. If you started on the rough grit side, you need to flip the stone over and follow the steps above again, including applying lubrication to the new side of the stone. After you complete these steps with this side, you'll have yourself a freshly sharpened knife to whittle with.

WHITTLING

Understanding Wood Grain

Wood grain can be difficult to wrap your head around if it's your first time learning about it. I find it useful to think of the human body first. Your body has all sorts of veins just under the surface that it uses to move blood and nutrients around. Trees also have veins and they are also just beneath the surface. But as trees grow, they become thicker. This happens from the outside rather than the inside. As trees develop another layer on their outside, the veins they were using become obsolete. The tree's veins begin to get blocked off and the tree stops using them as it develops more. When you cut into a tree and you see the grain, what you are seeing is the veins the tree no longer uses.

Wood grain is strongest when it is straight and we try to build our houses out of wood with a straight grain. But there are actually quite a few types of grain and each one can offer beauty to a project if you select it properly. We'll look at the different types of grain in just a moment. What's even more important to understand about grain is that the wood grain directly affects the texture of the wood itself. There is wood with a fine-texture and wood with a coarse-texture and this is determined by how the pores and cells of the wood have been laid out due to biology. If you hear someone say fine-grained when describing wood then they're referring to the texture of the wood rather than the grain itself because the grain directly affects the texture. Wood that has large cells is coarse. Small cells result in a fine wood and those in the middle are often considered fine. Although sometimes you'll see them referred to as moderately-grained or some variation.

The grain of each type of wood is extremely important to consider if you are going to be applying any kind of finish to your wood projects as the finish brings out the grains and makes them more prominent in appearance. This is often quite beautiful, especially if you've carefully considered how the grain will affect the end product ahead of time. When you're looking at a piece of wood that has been prepared and sold, then you'll be easily able to trace the lines of the grain and get a sense of how it will play into your project. But if you're working straight from the source with wood that hasn't been prepared, then you'll need to discover the grain for yourself by cutting into the wood.

When it comes to whittling, you'll find that it is easiest to make your cuts *with* the grain. When you cut along the grain you'll find that the wood peels away in a very smooth fashion. Cutting against the grain results in a much harder cut, as the wood is naturally going to have a certain level of resistance that you must overcome. Cutting against the grain will often lead to the wood splitting and this can be a nightmare that can easily ruin a project. It's almost always best to cut along the grain since it'll be easier and less likely to cause issues. But you shouldn't worry about it too much. In the beginning, you are almost certainly going to find yourself cutting against the grain by accident. This is just part of the learning experience. It may be frustrating but it will give you invaluable hands-on experience.

As for the different types of wood grain that you'll find, there's six. Straight grain runs vertically through the wood and is quite easy to understand. An irregular grain looks quite a bit like a straight grain but there is wobbling in the lines. You can think of a straight grain like a line drawn with a ruler and the irregular grain as a line drawn freehand. A diagonal grain is an especially beautiful type of grain which occurs when a straight grained wood is cut at an angle that isn't quite vertical. You can find a spiral grain in wood taken from trees that grew in a twisted direction. Interlocked grain occurs when the fibers of new layer growth occur in opposite directions. Finally, there is a wavy grain which looks similar to the irregular grain but happens because there is a constant change happening as the tree grows rather than an irregular change. Each of these types of grain can be used to make quite amazing wood carvings but working with each will require a few changes to your technique and where possible, I suggest beginners stick as close to a straight grain as they can.

WHITTLING

Safety Precautions

Whittling is all about carving wood with a knife and, therefore, it is incredibly important to have a quick discussion about safety. Poor knife handling can easily result in injury or death and that would be a tragedy. However, it isn't hard to be safe with a knife. It just takes a little bit of common sense and guidance. We're going to close out this chapter with our look at safety but before we get started, I want to highlight the fact that this is purely about being cautious. We're going to discuss mistakes in chapter three and these should also be read before you start any project. This section is about safety; that chapter will be about mistakes.

As far as safety goes, six key safety precautions that will make your whittling experience safe.

1 - Keep Your Blood Circle Clear: Sometimes called a safety circle, your blood circle is a term that comes from the Boy Scouts to describe the area around you that is in danger of being cut with your blade. Holding your knife in one hand, extend your arm out fully and turn in a circle. This gives you the size of the blood circle around you with you in the center of it. You want to keep your blood circle clear of any other people as they are at risk of being cut if something were to happen. I would go one step further and suggest that you keep your blood circle free from obstructions, if at all possible so that you don't accidentally bang your arm or your knife into any of your furniture.

2 - Keep Your Knife Outside of Your Blood Triangle: Your blood triangle is similar to your blood circle but it's about the risk you're in rather than anyone else. When you sit down, take a look at where your knees are and imagine that there is a line that connects them together. This space from your groin to your knees and the imaginary line between them is your blood triangle. It may feel the most comfortable to work inside of this space, as you'll find that the control you have over the blade is a little better (especially when beginning), but this is a very bad idea. When you work in this manner, you're getting the blade way too close to your femoral arteries and it'll only take one nasty slip to put your life at risk. Always keep the knife outside of your blood triangle.

3 - Cut Away From Your Body: This should be the most straight-forward tip and yet people seem to ignore it all the time. As you whittle something, you are cutting with the express purpose of removing some of the wood from the block you're cutting into. This means that the natural flow of whittling is that there will be resistance as the knife first cuts into the wood and then a release of that tension as the knife finishes the cut and removes the unwanted piece. The first part of the cut will be slow and sure and the last part is often pretty quick and explosive. If you're cutting towards yourself, you'll feel perfectly fine while the wood is resisting you but then one small mistake on the end of the cut and that blade is flying into your body. Always cut away from your body.

4 - Don't Reach for a Falling Knife: Never ever reach for a knife when it is falling. If a knife is falling, the right thing to do is move your body away from it. 99% of the time you'll have no issues. There is the small chance that you'll stab yourself in the foot but if you are moving away, the chances are so low that you're almost guaranteed not to have an issue. But if you react to dropping your knife by reaching to grab it, you've increased the chance of injury by a large degree. Right off the bat, there is the simple fact that you are no longer moving your body away from the knife. But now you're also moving your hand towards it. Do you think that you'll be able to grab only the handle? Chances aren't too good. More likely you'll grab the blade and cut or stab yourself on it. Rather than injuring your hands, just let the knife fall and pick it up after. All you lose is five seconds, that's a lot better than one of your five fingers.

5 - Use Small Cuts: When we were talking about cutting away from ourselves, we discussed the pressure that builds up in a cut. Well, the bigger the cut is, the more pressure there is going to be. More pressure means less control over the knife as it comes off the cut and ultimately less control over the cut itself, too. When it comes to knives, we should be all about control.

WHITTLING

Controlling your knife is the key to safety, after all. But there's another reason you should take small cuts; although, we'll save that reason for the chapter on common beginner mistakes.

6 - Always Close or Set Down Your Knife When You're Not Using It: This is another one of those straight-forward rules that seem to get ignored all too often. If you have finished using your knife, put it away. If it is a pocket knife, just flip the blade back down into the handle. If it's a speciality knife, slip the cover back over the blade. If you don't have a sheath or cover for your blade, you should make or buy one because it's a thousand times safer to put your blade away after you're done than to keep it out. In fact, saying "after you're done" is too loose of a term. If you are taking a break or even just stopping to chat, put that blade away so there are no accidents. It should be common sense.

Finally, while you don't necessarily need to invest in any particular safety equipment, it is a good idea, especially when beginning, to get a handy pair of heavy work gloves. This is especially important when you begin to practice pull cuts, which come toward your hand and body; the gloves can keep your hands safe from cuts. You might also consider investing in some clamps to be able to steady a project as you do detail work. These two minor investments will ensure that you follow all safety precautions to the best of your ability.

WHITTLING

20

WHITTLING

Chapter Summary

In order to get started with whittling, you need only understand a few basic materials, along with some safety protocols.

- The most important tool when whittling is the knife; choosing the right one is crucial.

- The second material you must have when whittling is, of course, the wood; again, choosing the right wood for each project is important for success.

- You should also know how to keep your knife sharp.

- Understanding wood grain is also essential for each project.

- Finally, following some basic safety precautions will ensure that nobody is injured in the process.

In the next chapter, you will learn the five major cuts used when whittling. With these five cuts, you will be able to whittle pretty much anything you want to but you will likely need lots of hands-on practice to perfect these techniques. To ensure that you are able to get the practice you need, we'll go through each of the cuts step-by-step.

CHAPTER TWO

WHITTLING CUTTING TECHNIQUES

Now that we've gotten our wood and our knife figured out it is time to start talking techniques. You might think that whittling is simply just cutting wood out of a stick but whittling is one of those deceptively simple practices. Technically, that is all there is to it. But there are five key cuts that we'll explore because not every cut is made the same way.

The cuts we'll discuss in this chapter are the straight rough cut, the push cut, the pull cut, the v-cut, and the stop cut. For the most part, these cuts are straightforward and easy to understand but don't worry if you don't quite get them at first. We'll start out by looking at these and then we'll go through them with step-by-step so you can practice them yourself. The first three cuts are easy to learn but the last two are going to take a bit more work because they are speciality cuts.

WHITTLING

The Straightaway Rough Cut

This cut is the easiest of the cuts because it's entire purpose is to remove a lot of wood at once. The reason it is called a rough cut is because you're getting the wood into roughly the right shape for the project you are working on. It is only appropriate for cutting the wood at the start of a project when it is still in a square, rectangle, or branch shape.

With this cut, we're looking to remove a bunch of wood at once but we never want to go too deeply. Going too deeply risks splitting the wood and this is almost always a bad thing to do. There are a few woodcarvers who are incredibly talented and know how to incorporate wood splitting into their projects but except for these few masters, it is universally bad to split your wood. It reduces the quality of the piece and can entirely destroy the progress you've made. With that said, it should be noted that if there was ever a time to split your wood, it would be while getting the rough shape into place since you haven't gotten to any of the intricate details yet. It can be a good idea to experiment with cuts of different depths in order to see what is acceptable and what risks splitting the wood.

Use this simple cut at the beginning with long cuts along the grain. To learn exactly how we pull this off, check out the step-by-step guide below.

WHITTLING

The Pull Cut

The pull cut is sometimes called the paring cut, the thumb cut, or the cut back. This is one of the more dangerous cuts in whittling and it actually contradicts one of our major safety rules. The pull cut is performed by pulling the knife towards yourself. The cut is done in a similar fashion to how you would pare an apple. We should cover a couple of safety matters. One is to use the pull cut while whittling outside of your blood triangle. Another is to angle it slightly so that the ultimate arc of the blade would be up and over your shoulder should it go flying. We also must be incredibly careful to keep each cut short and maintain total control by not being too fast with it. Finally, we can also wear some thumb or hand protection to reduce the risk even further. When following these safety precautions, the pull cut is no more dangerous than any other cut.

But what the pull cut is great for is control. It is much easier to control a knife that is being pulled compared to one that is being pushed, which is the next cut we'll be looking at. This makes the pull cut fantastic for carving details. The level of control you have over the pull cut is so great that it is the most commonly used cut used when whittling. So expect to be making use of it quite often, just don't forget your safety measures.

WHITTLING

The Push Cut

The pull cut is the most commonly used cut in whittling but it isn't always possible to get the knife into the position to be able to pull. Sometimes, you simply have to cut something that the pull won't reach. In those cases, we often need to use the push cut. As the name suggests, this cut is achieved by pushing the blade. This makes it a much safer cut compared to the pull cut; although, you'll still want to be well outside of your blood triangle. The trade-off is that it is a little harder to control on the dismount. Getting the blade where you want it and applying the right amount of force to whittle away at the wood isn't a hassle but it can be easy to apply too much force so that you lose control of the blade as it leaves the wood.

But if you can get the right amount of force so that you don't have problems dismounting, you will find that the push cut offers nearly as much control as the pull cut does. Together the pull cut and the push cut will be your most used cuts. You'll start your project with your straight away rough cuts and then you'll turn to pull and push cutting to start bringing the piece together. From there, we need to move into more detailed and specific cuts in order to bring out textures such as hair.

The V-Cut

The V-cut, as with the stop cut (as we will next discuss), incorporates two cuts into the project in order to create the effect. They are incredibly similar to each other but they each have a different effect on the final project that must be considered in full. When you are using a pull cut or a push cut, you are removing wood off the top side of the block or branch. Let's pretend we're trying to carve some type of face and we want to do the ears. We can whittle away at them with a push or pull cut but we'd have an incredibly difficult time defining them as ears. If you look at a person's ears you'll see the way that they come out from the body. But if you were to whittle ears with the push or pull cut then they would still be flat against the head. Or think about how hair looks. If you're trying to whittle hair, you'd want some definition showing the different locks; otherwise, it wouldn't look real. But separating the locks from each other runs into the same problem that separating the ear from the body does. We simply can't achieve the right effect with the previous cuts. That's why we need to use a v-cut.

A v-cut, also known as v-notching, is a technique that requires you to make two cuts. In doing so, you'll remove a little triangle piece of wood and thereby create a notch to create separation. If you made this cut on the surface of a piece of flat wood, it would look like a diagonal incline that leads down into the wood until it comes upon a nearly identical incline leading back out. If you were trying to do ears or separate fingers then this v-shaped notch would be perfect.

But not every notch needs to be v-shaped. Sometimes we only want a single inclined surface rather than two. For the other kind of notch we use in whittling, we need to learn the stop cut.

The Stop Cut

As mentioned, the stop cut is a variation of the v-cut. Or maybe the v-cut is a variation of the stop cut; it really doesn't matter. What matters is that these two cuts are what we use to notch the wood we're whittling and if we don't understand the difference between the two of them, we'll find ourselves constantly selecting the wrong cut for the job at hand.

The v-cut creates a notch that has almost identical slopes in and out of it which help to give definition to a project and create separation. We considered how it worked for ears but now let's try to picture working on a chin. If you were to create the separation between a person's neck and their chin with a v-cut then you would end up with a weird figure that just doesn't look right. This is because our chins don't function this way. A person's chin almost hangs over their neck, just barely. But because we're typically eye-level with people we see, the chin blocks the neck from view. If we want to recreate this effect with wood, then a v-cut won't work because a v-cut is perfectly visible; there would be no overhanging effect.

We use a stop cut for this effect. A stop cut creates a notch that inclines down into the wood and then stops abruptly. Rather than an identical incline coming out of the wood there is just a straight line back up to the top of the wood. If looked at from the right angle, then the lowest point of the incline would be bathed in shadow from the wood seemingly overhanging it. If you don't quite follow, don't sweat it. We're moving now to our step-by-step practice and that'll make it easier to understand.

Step-by-Step: The Straightaway Rough Cut

The straightaway rough cut is the easiest of the cuts to understand and perform because it is purposefully rough.

Begin by taking the wood in your hand and holding it outside of your blood triangle.

With the knife in your other hand, use long sweeps along the grain. These sweeps should be pointed away from you, similar to the push cut except that you aren't going to push the blade with a finger. Simply hold the blade, let it cut into the wood as much as it will take and carry it through to the end. Again, these rough cuts are along the grain.

This is all there is to the cut but you should always hold the knife securely in your hand, all five fingers holding on tight. You must always cut along the grain. If you try to force the blade into the wood too much, it will split so take multiple cuts rather than trying to get everything done at once.

WHITTLING

Step-by-Step: The Pull Cut

The pull cut is the one in which you pull the blade towards your body so you must approach this cut with caution. Yes, it is the most common cut in whittling but it is also the most dangerous in terms of possible harm and thus you should never use it mindlessly.

Start by taking the piece of wood in your off-hand. The side which you want to whittle from is turned upwards, your hand supporting the wood from the bottom. Keep your knife in your right, or dominant, hand. You want to ensure that the wood is held securely so wrap your thumb around the side of it so that it doesn't wiggle in your grasp.

With your knife hand, use your thumb to hold the end of the wood in place while you use your other fingers to hold the blade. You want to take short, controlled cuts so you should only be carving near the end of the piece of wood.

Pull the blade towards yourself using your four fingers in a pulling motion while your thumb braces the wood with a pushing force. We call this cut the pull cut because the blade is pulled but your blade hand actually manages both to pull and push at the same time.

WHITTLING

Step-by-Step: The Push Cut

For the push cut, you will want to be especially careful to work outside of your blood triangle and with a clear blood circle. You should do this at all times, of course, but beginners are explicitly advised to listen as it's easy to lose control of the knife at this stage if you're not careful.

Take the piece of wood you're working on in your non-dominant hand and hold it similarly to the pull cut. With the pull cut, we hold the wood like an apple and focus on the bottom side of it. For the push cut, we'll hold the wood like an apple but we cut from the top end. This means we're cutting away from ourselves and the danger of losing control is in accidentally harming another person.

Use your dominant hand to position the blade on the wood, cutting with the grain. Hold the knife so that your fingers are around the handle and your thumb is holding the back of the blade firm and steady. With your hand holding the wood, use the thumb along the end of the blade so it is supported along the body. This will allow you to keep a steady cut and easily glide through the wood as you are whittling. Remember not to push the knife too deep into the wood since there is a chance of splitting.

Step-by-Step: The V-Cut

The v-cut uses a combination of the push and pull cuts. As such, it means that you are going to need to hold the wood like you did for those cuts. When making the push cut, you'll hold the wood in a position where you can push the blade with your off-hand thumb. When making the pull cut, you'll hold the wood like an apple and use your dominant hand's thumb to leverage against the wood.

It doesn't matter which cut you make first; that's entirely up to your own personal taste. We'll start with the pull cut because it is a little bit easier. Since we want to cut a v-shape out of the wood, we need to dig into the wood a little bit more than we normally would. This means there is a much higher chance of splitting the wood, especially when you are beginning. Generally, just try not to go too deep but I recommend that you practice on some scrap wood to find the depth at which splits seem to start to occur and then experiment with cuts from there.

The first cut only digs into the wood a little bit. It comes towards you but moves down at an angle to dig into the wood. You need to remove the knife by pulling it back out of the cut you made rather than trying to change direction from inside. You'll ruin the cut if you try to change at this point so remove the blade back the way it came and switch your stance to push cutting.

WHITTLING

Position the blade at the same angle that you used when pull cutting. Keep the blade steady and push down until the two cuts meet each other and a v-shaped wood chip is carved out.

Step-by-Step: The Stop Cut

Our final cut is not too different from the v-cut. We're going to use both wood grips but our pull cut is going to be different. Take your blade in your hand for a pull cut.

Instead of going in at an angle that pulls towards you, just make your blade at a 90-degree angle to the wood and cut straight down into it. You can and should use your thumb on the end of the knife to make the cut as steady as possible. Going too deep will split the wood so I recommend experimenting with the stop cut on some scrap wood. Be extremely careful to remove the blade the same way it came. This is even more important with the stop cut than it is with the v-cut.

Next, take your blade and switch to the push cut stance. Don't forget to cut outside of your blood triangle. Make a push cut into the wood so that the cut connects with the lowest part of the previous cut. This action will create an oddly shaped triangle wedge you're removing. It's called a stop cut because this cut hits a wall, the other cut, and stops. It makes a much shaper wedge than the v-cut. To get a better sense of both of these, try practicing them and then comparing the removed wedges to see how they differ from one another.

With that, you now know how to do the five key cuts that we'll use.

WHITTLING

Chapter Summary

This chapter covers the basic whittling cuts: the straight rough cut, the push cut, the pull cut, the v-cut, and the stop cut. It also provides step-by-step instructions as to how to employ these cuts.

- The straight rough cut is the easiest of the cuts because its entire purpose is to remove a lot of wood at once.

- The pull cut is sometimes called the paring cut, the thumb cut, or the cut back. It should be undertaken with caution as it can be dangerous, pulling the knife toward your hand.

- The push cut is used when it isn't possible to get the knife into the position to be able to pull.

- A v-cut, also known as v-notching, is a technique that requires you to make two cuts. In doing so, you'll remove a little triangle piece of wood and thereby create a notch to create separation.

- A stop cut creates a notch that inclines down into the wood and then stops abruptly.

- Follow the step-by-step instructions to learn each of these cuts in turn.

In the next chapter, you will learn about the most common mistakes that beginners make when whittling.

WHITTLING

Issues such as cutting too deeply and splitting the wood or carving with a dull knife are common mistakes that beginners find themselves committing. By learning the mistakes before you commit them, you can, hopefully, avoid them – or at least know how to recover from them if you make them yourself.

CHAPTER THREE

COMMON MISTAKES TO AVOID BEFORE YOU START

Mistakes are all too common when a beginner starts whittling. Realistically, mistakes are all too common when a beginner starts anything. It doesn't matter if it is whittling, cooking, writing or knitting. Mistakes and beginners go hand-in-hand.

Many people, themselves primarily beginners, find this to be a frustrating relationship because nobody really wants to go out and make mistakes. People get into something like whittling because they've seen something cool that was made with it or they get their hands on a book like this that is filled with awesome projects to create and they want to experience that joy of creation. A mistake along the way can deeply worry someone. Mistakes can even discourage people and convince them that they shouldn't be whittling.

But mistakes themselves aren't the problem. We'll look at just how important mistakes are in a little bit so you can see that mistakes aren't problematic. They help us to understand what we can improve and what we are doing well. Yet there are plenty of mistakes that we don't want to make because they set us back, risk our health or the integrity of our projects. If we can avoid mistakes of this nature, then we can save ourselves a lot of time. But just how do we identify a common mistake?

Thankfully, we live in the age of the internet where we can go onto whittling message boards to speak with professional and novice woodcarvers alike. We can watch videos on YouTube to improve our skills and avoid mistakes. We have never had a larger resource for whittling than we do now with the internet. The mistakes in this chapter come from a combination of personal experience and message board conversations with whittlers that have been at it for years. These are only the most common mistakes, mistakes that you can learn to avoid by studying this chapter. There will always be more mistakes to be made. Even experts continue to discover new mistakes. I recommend that you consider this chapter a primer on your earliest mistakes and I recommend that you turn to a message board such as that on WoodCarvingIllustrated.com to seek further help, make friends that share your interest, and join the community of whittlers and wood carvers from all over the world.

WHITTLING

Only Work With Good Lighting

Working with good lighting is one of those elements which seems to go against the culturally-held image of whittling. If you ask someone to tell you what whittling looks like, there is an incredibly high chance that they mention carving a block of wood around a campfire. The image has been burnt into the Western brain thanks to movies and television and it is one of the places where it is enjoyable to whittle.

But you wouldn't want to whittle around the campfire if the sun has gone down completely. There just wouldn't be enough light. You need a decent amount of light to be able to see the wood you are working on. The lower the quality of the light you are using, the higher the number of mistakes you'll find yourself making. Nicks have a way of accumulating in those areas where the shadows are the deepest and you can't fully see what you're doing. Enough mistakes result in a failed project and you having to start over again with a new piece of wood.

Always ensure that you have proper lighting when you are whittling so you can see all the nooks and crannies of your wood and ensure that your cuts are accurate and properly placed.

WHITTLING

Never Whittle With a Dull Knife

Whittling with a dull knife is a rookie mistake and one that has multiple negative effects associated with it. The first and most important effect is related to safety. A dull blade is not going to cut very well and so it is likely to get caught in the wood and require extra force to remove it. This extra force increases the risk of self-harm and harm to those in your blood circle. Cutting with a dull knife could be considered a safety hazard to avoid but that alone isn't why it landed on this list.

If we set safety aside, then cutting with a dull knife is a rookie mistake because it will result in sloppier cuts and it increases the chances of splitting the wood. The first comes from the fact that the blade is no longer cutting through the wood. A sharp blade slices right through the wood. You can tell a cut made with a sharp knife because it will be uniform and smooth. A dull blade doesn't slice at all but rather it tears into the wood and this means it produces a cut that is uneven and rough. A cut with a dull knife results in a cut that you can't fully control. Typically, a knife isn't uniformly dull as different sections of the blade will dull sooner than others and this goes a long way towards explaining why a dull cut can be odd.

WHITTLING

When you take the time to sharpen your knife, you are ensuring that the entire blade is sharpened and brought back up to full health, as it were. This means that the uneven dull blade is transformed into an even and sharp blade and you can stop tearing at the wood and start slicing through it again instead. If you aren't sure if your blade is dull before you begin whittling, take a few minutes to sharpen it. By sharpening the blade first, before making any cuts, you retain complete control over the whittling experience and the project at hand.

Choose the Right Wood

It is important to choose the right wood for whatever project you start. Woods with heavy grains or hardwoods are the hardest for a beginner. Try to choose wood that has a straight grain, as it is the simplest to carve. As suggested in chapter one, balsa or basswood are the best choices for beginners. Of course, you can certainly carve with twigs or branches that you can collect – for free – in your backyard; however, make sure you test out the strength and quality of the wood before you commit to your project. "Found" wood like this can be a cheap way in which to test your skills if you exercise safety precautions; if you mess up the project, you can start over with no loss of investment. As mentioned previously, softwoods are best for beginners.

Also, consider the difference between green (fresh) wood and dried wood: if you are picking up found wood in your backyard, this will typically be green wood. It is softer and thus easier to carve; however, because of its pliability, it doesn't absorb many mistakes before falling apart. Dried woods are better for more advanced projects, but they are harder to carve. Dried woods are what you would seek out in a woodshop or other outdoors equipment store.

Don't Whittle While Tired

Being tired is a heck of a lot worse for us than we consider it to be. More accidents happen on the road due to being tired than anything else. Film schools teach whole classes about how dangerous it is to over work yourself into a state of exhaustion on a set because the accident rate increases in direct proportion to the extra hours the crew puts in. Being tired isn't just uncomfortable, it is deadly because of the way we convince ourselves that we're still fully capable of what we were capable of doing while wide awake.

Whittling is no exception. When you whittle, you should be awake and cognizant. To whittle when you are tired is to invite accidents. Most of these accidents will result in damage to the wood. A split here, a piece taken off by accident there. But the risk of harming yourself or others goes up dramatically the more tired you are. If you want to avoid injuring yourself or the people around

WHITTLING

you, then you absolutely must not whittle when you are tired. Simply don't whittle when you're tired because it means more mistakes and lower quality work.

WHITTLING

Chapter Summary

All beginners make mistakes when embarking on a new hobby; whittling is no exception. Here you will find some common mistakes to avoid.

- Whittle under the right lighting; you want to be able to see clearly.

- Never whittle with a dull knife. Contrary to conventional wisdom, a dull knife is much more likely to cause injury than a sharp one.

- Choose the right wood for your project; softwoods are best for beginners.

- Don't whittle when tired! You are much more likely to make mistakes or even injure yourself.

In the next chapter, you will learn how to start whittling for yourself with projects selected specifically for beginners. These projects will be a great way to start trying your hand at whittling while still creating unique trinkets and figures that you can feel proud of. Consider these projects an on-ramp for those to come in chapter five.

CHAPTER FOUR

FUN PROJECTS FOR BEGINNERS

Now that you have a clear idea of what you need in the way of simple tools and appropriate wood, you can embark on projects that will help you hone your skills. These projects are grouped into categories below with some suggestions on specific projects you can try within these categories. Depending on what your purpose is in whittling – creating unique gifts for others, providing yourself with a fun hobby, or making practical objects in affordable ways – you should be able to find a project that is well-suited to your skills and your needs. The descriptions below will give you an idea of how to get started with each project; although, you might also want to seek out some visual assistance, such as diagrams or videos for some of the more complicated projects. The ideas contained within this chapter and the next are designed to get you started and to allow you to unleash your own creativity. As with most hobbies, we learn by doing, through trial and error, so you only need to find some time and space in which to get whittling to become an expert!

Many practiced whittlers suggest that you begin at the very beginning with your first project, and try your hand at a wooden egg as a test run: this project teaches you a lot about wood grain and how to work it properly with your knife. It is also instrumental in teaching you better knife skills, by learning to round and shape an object. It also assists you in building hand strength, which you will need as you start to embark on more complex projects. Here is a brief step-by-step guide to whittling a wooden egg:

- Divide your block of wood into thirds on all four sides.

- Decide which end will be the broad end of the egg and mark that more heavily with your pencil.

- Start with the broad end, slice off the corners, and start to round that end using a pull cut parallel to the wood grain.

- Rotate your block as you work, rounding out the broad end slowly (rather than one side at a time; this helps create a balanced effect).

- Now, slice off the corners at the tapered end, and begin rounding off there. Your block of wood, at this point, should look like a cylinder.

WHITTLING

- Then, start to shape your cylinder into the final oval egg form by making cuts at an angle to the grain, using both push and pull cuts to smooth out the egg shape. Start slowly and carefully, and if your cut splits rather than slices through the wood, change the direction of the cut.

- Continue to round out the egg, using finer and finer cuts as you get closer to finishing.

- Clean up the surface of the egg by sanding if you like (leaving the cuts in the egg is also fine for a more rustic look). Erase any pencil marks if necessary.

- Finally, to seal the surface, you can spray or paint on some clear lacquer or you can decide to paint and seal the egg. Adding a final coat of wax to the egg will give it a nice glow as well.

WHITTLING

Remember, in this or any project, to follow basic safety precautions as detailed in chapter one. In addition to practicing safe knife habits, you might also consider wearing eye protection (it's a rare but potential hazard of getting splinters to the eye) and when applying lacquer or paint, be sure to do this in a well-ventilated area. See below for some more ideas on various beginner's projects.

Animal Animations

Animal carvings are among some of the most popular wood crafting projects that are available to whittlers. These make lovely personal gifts as well as unique home décor. You could even start a collection or make a keepsake for family and friends. In any case, when starting with animal projects, it is best to think of them as simple figurines. When you get more skilled, you can begin to endow your animal projects with more details and realism. For a beginning project, simply think about the abstract lines needed to provide an impressionistic sense of the animal. Follow these basic guidelines when making animal figures:

- Find a picture of the animal you want to carve, or better yet, a picture of another carver's basic animal figure to help you determine your basic lines.

- Mark your block of wood with pencil, making a sketch of the basic lines of the animal.

- Start by removing bits of wood that will be unnecessary to the final shape: for example, cut away the wood between the ears of a rabbit or between the legs and tail of a dog.

WHITTLING

- Then, begin the careful work of cutting and shaving off around your drawing in order to create the simple shape of your chosen animal.

- After you have your simple shape, then you can add fine details using smaller and sharper knives if you like (adding whiskers, for example, or eyes); although, this is more advanced work.

- As with the wooden egg, smooth over the rough edges, if you choose, and seal with lacquer, paint, or wax.

Some other basic tips when whittling animal figures (or any larger figurines) are as follows: you might consider using clamps to hold the figure in place so you can free up both of your hands; this is not required, but it can be helpful when first learning to carve lines. Use stop cuts to designate the different boundaries within the figure before you begin the detail work (mark the boundary between head and neck, neck and body, body and tail, and so on).

With beginning animal projects, again think about making an abstract representation of the animal rather than a fully realistic example. Rather than carving, say, a particular breed of dog, simply contour the shape of a sitting dog or, slightly more complex, a dog howling. Cats and rabbits are also some of the easier projects to start with, as they have distinctive but simple body parts that make them easily recognizable even if your carving isn't exactly to scale; the long tail and rounded face with pointed ears of the cat are fairly distinguishable, while the long ears and rounded tail of the bunny are also easily rendered in abstract form. Certain kinds of birds lend themselves to abstract representation, as well, such as owls with their distinctive geometric shape and ducks with their recognizable bills. Think of making a wood representation out of a rubber ducky, and you get the idea.

Flights of Fancy

Along with animal projects, carving fantastical little men is another hallmark of the whittling community. These little wizards and gnomes, as well as other fantastical creatures, can be simple beginning projects. Again, like the animal abstractions described in the previous section, the characteristic features of particular

WHITTLING

fantasy figures are easily discerned, so they don't necessarily require great detail or expert skill in order to make them recognizable and fun. Follow these steps below to make a very simple wizard figure, identifiable by his pointy wizard hat and long beard:

- You only need a wood carving knife, a pencil, and a rectangular block of wood for this project (something small, about five or six inches long).

- Now, mark the point where the hat will end with a horizontal line about an inch from one end of your block of wood.

- Then mark a second line on the diagonal, down from the point of your horizontal line to the edge of the wood on both sides. This will end up being the starting point of the face.

- Next, make a stop cut on the diagonal lines, and carve out a small area (about ⅛") below the stop cuts.

- Go down another ⅛ to ¼" and make a clear short cut horizontally for the nose (picture that you are carving the wizard from a side view). Carve out a triangle underneath this cut to make the nose stand out in relief.

- Then, carve out two triangular eyes above the nose; at the bridge of the nose, make two

WHITTLING

diagonal cuts going away and down from the nose on each side.

- From the triangle under the nose, draw two long lines on each side to represent a long mustache, then carve out those lines to give it a three-dimensional appearance (as you did with the triangle under the nose).

- Next, draw on the beard and remove the rectangular part of the wood around the beard to make it come down to a clear point.

- Now, return to the hat: go back to your very first cut and make another cut a bit above it for the rim of the hat. Then, cut off the rectangular parts of the wood to make the hat come into its distinctive point at the top.

- Finally, smooth out any rough edges and seal or paint your figure.

This simple wizard's face is a perfect beginner's project for the hobbyist; for a more advanced project, you can learn how to make a standing figurine, body and all (look to the following chapter for this more advanced project). This same procedure can be slightly modified, of course, for it to look more like a gnome-type figure or a simple old man face.

Other possibilities for fantasy projects include the ever-popular Star Wars character Yoda; with his

WHITTLING

distinctive ears and diminutive frame, a wooden facsimile of Yoda can be achieved by a beginning whittler. Just start by drawing or transferring the simplest image you can find of Yoda—maybe start with just the head—and work around your block.

Another simple figurine for beginners is the dinosaur: again, think of the abstract representation of identifiable dinosaurs and work from there: the brontosaurus with its long neck and short legs is a simple one to start with, as is the T-Rex with its long body, broad head, and tiny arms.

Basically, when you are considering beginner's projects, especially of figures (whether real or imaginary), think about the basic abstract features, the simple geometric lines that will identify the object. Once you become comfortable with these basics, you can easily start to add detail and complexity to them. But these basic figures are also quite appealing and beautiful in their own right.

Also consider focusing your attention on just one aspect of the figure you wish to carve, such as the wizard's face above or just the head of Yoda, rather than a fully realized figurine; one element is complex enough to tackle for a beginner. Practicing on each part of the body, using the simplest geometric patterns, will allow you to develop greater skills as you work (not to mention patience). This advice is similar to that given to novice

WHITTLING

illustrators or painters: find the geometric patterns in each figure you wish to reproduce before you get started; working with simple circles, squares, triangles, and the like will sharpen your abilities and prepare you for more complicated projects. As you start each project, try to distill it down to its most basic essence. This will leave you with more success and less frustration in the end.

Games Galore

Other popular projects for whittlers include simple toys; this is a way in which your hobby can become a family legacy, passing down handmade objects to children and grandchildren. While the kiddos may not appreciate the time and thought that goes into a hand-carved wooden toy when they are young, they will certainly grow up to understand the love and thoughtfulness that goes into such a project. This is also a way of teaching kids the value of simplicity, of hard work and commitment, and of maintaining particular traditions. With our increasing reliance on technology for our entertainment (not to mention almost every other aspect of our daily lives, such as work and home upkeep), we often overlook the notable value in the handmade and the beauty of the simple. Creating basic toys for your children, grandchildren, nieces, nephews, and friends of the family is about more than just making an object; it's about affirming a particular way of engaging in the world. If you have children in your life that are old enough to handle a knife with care, then this might also be a wonderful way to share quality time with them.

Some of the beginning projects that you can try out in this category are super simple block toys, for one, or basic chess pieces for older children. You can also find a whole host of ideas about carving simple trains or cars, and the animal figures that were discussed previously can also be conceived of as toys: making an entire train or creating a menagerie of animals is a way in which you can create a yearly birthday tradition; each year, you craft a new car for the train or a new animal for the group. These kinds of toys can also be fertile ground for developing the imagination, wherein you can dream up all kinds of scenarios for where the train is going and why, or for how the animals set out together on an adventure, *Wind in the Willows*-style. These can become traditions that enrich a relationship with memories that last a lifetime!

Step-by-step instructions for carving something like a train car are very straightforward: a train is essentially a geometric figure, a rectangle body with circle wheels and a triangular chimney at the top of the train with perhaps a triangular headlight jutting out from the front or rectangular windows cut out in relief on subsequent cars. For a beginner, you might even consider carving the body of the train and adding already formed wheels to it; this will give you the confidence you need to

WHITTLING

challenge yourself with more complex projects further down the line. Also think about working with the various parts of the project, rather than carving the entire train out of one large block of wood: that is, carve the body, then carve the simple chimney and headlight out of other blocks of wood, using strong wood glue to pull the toy together. Clearly, carving the entirety out of one block of wood will ensure that it is sturdier, but as a beginner, you might want to work up to that. Eventually, you might end up with a long train of cars, ferrying a whole host of circus animals to the next town! Start small, gain confidence, and then use your imagination to broaden the scope of your project as you see fit.

Another relatively straightforward project would be to make chess pieces – as simple or as complex as your skills will allow – for a personalized set. While you can

WHITTLING

look to a traditional chess set as inspiration, some of the techniques that you might have to use, say, to carve a knight atop a horse are perhaps too advanced. Again, as with previous projects, think about how to make the figures representative of their roles in chess – queen, king, rook, bishop, knight, and pawn – in abstract and simple ways. Obviously, one way to differentiate the various pieces, while also denoting their importance, is to vary the height; the king and queen should be tallest, of course, with pawns the shortest, as in a classic set. Then, simply think of how to identify each piece by one identifying feature: a crown for the queen and king (with some distinguishing mark between them), a basic tower for the rooks, a staff for the bishops, a sword or shield for the knights, and an abstract shape for the pawns. The pawns could simply be small rectangular pieces of wood that you round at the top or carve some simple design into. Again, as with the train, this could be a project that extends over the years, while you add to your collection over time. Once you start to gain confidence in your skills, you might decide to make chess pieces according to a theme or style; for example, you can stylize your chess pieces as medieval-looking figurines, similar to the wizard face from the previous section with a solid base on which to rest or you could riff on a Tiki-themed set, as shown on the LSIrish.com site. While these would be more complex than the very basic abstract representations that you might start with, they still rely on basic geometric shapes in order to create a more unique quality. Again, your only limitations are your imagination and your evolving skills.

Finally, perhaps the easiest of all is to find some square blocks of wood and practice carving letters and numbers into all sides of them, making decorative borders around the letter or number as your skill level allows. Using stencils to draw the letters and numbers onto the block makes for simple carving, and you can make an extraordinarily thoughtful and instructive gift for a friend or family member's small child. You can either cut the letter or number *into* the block of wood, or carve *around* the letter or number so it stands out, whichever proves most comfortable to you. When you finish these, be sure to sand the blocks down, and paint or seal them well, so the little ones don't get splinters or cuts from rough edges.

Holiday Hobbies

There are all sorts of holiday projects that you can carve for display or for gifts; again, these kinds of projects can be a yearly reminder of keeping up with your hobby, maintaining a tradition over time. Each year you can remind yourself to work on another simple (or increasingly complex) project to add to your collection.

For example, you can whittle some simple hearts for Valentine's Day. For a beginner's take on the project, think of the hearts not as three-dimensional objects but rather as flat, two-dimensional shapes that you carve into a small block of wood. Making rounded carvings is hard enough in two-dimensional shapes, of course, so work your way up to carving a fully heart-shaped object. Basically, all you need to do for this is to draw a heart shape on a block of wood, then cut around the drawing; then, decide whether to remove the wood from inside the shape (creating a heart design recessed in the wood) or to remove the wood from the outside of the shape (creating a heart that stands out from the wood). In the first case, you have essentially carved a cookie cutter, which you can use to press out heart shapes in soft materials like dough. In the second case, you have essentially created a stamp, where you can ink the heart and make impressions on other materials such as paper. Or you can treat the two-dimensional heart as a decorative object in and of itself, making a simple border, and painting or sealing it when finished. This kind of project could be conceived of as an elaborate Valentine's Day card to a loved one – certainly a personal project that will endear you to anyone's heart.

WHITTLING

The same kind of principle can be applied to making a wooden carving of the American flag for Independence Day. Again, the flag is essentially a compilation of geometric shapes – rectangles, squares, and stars. This is a project that can be scaled up in size without gaining in complexity to make a lawn-sized display if you like (though it might require larger tools of an electronic persuasion). In any case, you can easily carve out a flag design onto a block of wood and paint it accordingly for Fourth of July celebrations. Think about carving a set of small flags to use as place settings for a holiday meal or as weights to hold down paper products on a picnic. These are lovely ways to showcase your woodworking ability.

The Christmas holidays, of course, lend themselves to all sorts of decorations, and you can employ your new-found hobby in creating something unique and

WHITTLING

personal for your home. One of the simplest projects you can do is to make a Santa face: follow the instructions for the wizard project as detailed above, but soften the sharp edges of the beard and hat to make the figure more Santa-like. With the right application of paint, your Santa face can be a festive addition to any holiday display, or, if you happen to have a drill, turned into an ornament to hang on the tree. Just drill a small hole at the top of Santa's hat and use a loop of red or green ribbon to hang it from your Christmas tree.

A cartoon-style reindeer face is also a fairly simple carving project that can be turned into a companion decoration or ornament. In fact, you could eventually produce enough small, simple carvings to fill an entire tree if you get immersed in the project over time. These could also be "collector's" items among your friends and family, sentimental reminders of holidays spent together in the past.

Finally, follow these simple steps below to create a jack-o-lantern for the Halloween holidays. It can be used, as the example with the heart above, as a kind of cookie cutter (more effective if you are able to remove most or all of the wood around the cut-out, which might require more expensive and specialized tools) or as a cool decoration for a Halloween display. Think about the process of carving a pumpkin, something that most of us have tried our hand at one time or another; now, just transfer that geometric simplicity to wood.

WHITTLING

- Always begin with a drawing. Again using simple geometric shapes to get you started. It's best to sketch it out on paper before drawing directly to the wood, so that you can correct any mistakes or change any details before you get started cutting.

- Once you have your jack-o-lantern face ready to go, trace it onto the wood, then start cutting around the obvious bits, creating simple triangles for eyes and nose, then cutting out your jagged-tooth mouth – the familiar shape of a basic jack-o-lantern look.

- Now that you've carved out the shape of the pumpkin, you need to start removing the wood around its features in order to make the shape stand out. As with much of the work in whittling, it comes down to removing wood as much as shaping it. Gently work your way around the eyes, nose, and mouth, removing the wood until the face stands out from the block.

- If you have additional tools, such as a gouge tool or a v-parting chisel, you can get in closer around the features to make them pronounced and clear. But it's not required.

- Be sure to carve around the pumpkin, too, so that the face is centered on a round or oval template, rather than floating above the wood without boundaries.

- Once you feel your jack-o-lantern is in clear relief, you can either cut around the figure to complete the process of making it into a usable cookie cutter (the best equipment for this would be a jigsaw tool, so this moves you beyond simple whittling) or you could paint the pumpkin for use in a holiday display. In that case, think about additional but simple details you could add, such as a stem – green to contrast with the orange of the pumpkin and the black of the face – or more detail to the eyes, such as pupils.

Home and Garden Décor

Certainly, your new-found hobby of whittling can also be applied to practical creations, such as items for

WHITTLING

your home and garden. Any of the holiday crafts that you make, of course, can be used as décor, so use your imagination to think about other objects that might brighten up your living room or your garden with your own personal touch. Making picture frames or display cabinets takes you somewhat out of the realm of whittling – these kinds of projects require hammers, nails, industrial glue and the like – they are still firmly within the realm of DIY woodworking and require some of the basic skills of whittling. You can also think of projects wherein you are adding décor to purchased frames and such: using small pieces of scrap wood, practice whittling simple shapes and symbols that you can glue to existing frames or other furniture. Think of hearts, flowers or leaves, symbols such as a peace sign, or small abstract animals – whatever you think captures your style and interests. This is a great way to get in some good practice without wasting wood; using leftover scraps of wood for small projects is an excellent way to try out something new. Always start with a drawing to help orient your project, and then allow yourself to push the limits of your skills. This is how you will be able to move from novice to expert over time. Once you start to feel more confident in your skills, you might be bold enough to move onto other household items with larger impact. Also, think about how your small animal carvings (or holiday ideas) can be scaled up for outdoor display.

WHITTLING

While a lawn gnome isn't a necessary addition to your yard, it happens to be one of the most popular projects among woodworkers. It appears on almost every beginning whittler's list; certainly, this is due to the quirky appeal of the lawn gnome, but it is also likely due to the fact that this little project tests all of your emerging skills and allows you to customize your project based on your own creativity. While it would be difficult to convey how to whittle a lawn gnome without accompanying pictures, here is a basic set of instructions to get you started:

- You want a decent-sized block of wood to begin, something about a foot long and at least two inches deep; the length allows you to exaggerate the hat or the beard of the gnome.

- Start by making centerlines around the entire piece, as you want to make sure to maintain perspective as you begin your cuts. Then, mark a line about four inches up from the bottom to designate the body of the gnome; the remaining length is for the hat (or reverse, and make a short hat and a long gnome beard).

- Make another line about an inch up from the bottom, again all the way around your block, to see where the hands will be in front and the bottom will be in the back. Then, measure about two and a half inches from the bottom to mark where the end of the nose will be.

WHITTLING

- Once you have all of these measurements in place, you will be able to see how the gnome will eventually be proportioned. Make notes for yourself in pencil, if you need a reminder as to what each line denotes.

- Start with the gnome itself, carving away some of the wood below the hat line so you can mark where the face will be: again, you can use your own creative discretion in making the face. Many gnome projects don't have eyes – the hat comes down over them – because eyes can be tricky to make. Whatever you decide, draw the face on the wood carved out from under the hat line before you start to carve.

- Make a stop cut at the bottom of the nose and continue carving until the nose stands out; this is a distinctive feature of the lawn gnome, the protruding nose.

- Once the nose is in place, make a stop cut above the nose at a downward angle on each side: these will be your eyebrows. Then, cut upward from the bridge of your nose to the eyebrow to delineate the cheekbones. Fill the face in with other details, if you like.

- Return to your line for the hands in the front and the bottom in the back, and make a stop cut there. The idea is to have the hands "clasped" together in the front (all you need do is make some small cuts there to denote separate hands and fingers), while a small cut vertically in the back delineates the bottom.

- Finally, return to the hat: this can be as elaborate or as simple as your skills and your desires dictate: carve some swirling grooves all the way up to the top, or simply make the hat a tall and pointed affair with perhaps some simple designs gently carved in.

- As you are working on the hat, make sure to prop your gnome up on his feet to ensure that your project maintains the necessary balance to remain upright. The hat must be carved away enough so that it doesn't pull the gnome over. This takes some practice but is well worth the effort. Soon, you'll be making enough lawn gnomes for all your neighbors!

Lettered Messages

Another type of project that you can undertake is to carve letters into wood, which seems easy but does require a little bit of skill and some patience. Carving letters into wood may not technically be whittling but it is adjacent to whittling and can help you develop skills of precision that can be utilized in other projects. In this beginning phase, you are just looking to carve out letters in relief onto a wood surface (rather than carving a three-dimensional letter itself). Developing this skill allows you to personalize your projects, of course, as well as making practical or whimsical signage for your home or shop.

The first step is always to draw the lettering onto the wood before you get started (and be sure to use a soft wood like balsa or basswood for this project). There are several ways in which you can do this: you can use a stencil to trace letters onto your wood; you can use carbon paper to transfer lettering to the wood if you don't have a stencil for what you want or you can draw the lettering free-hand if you have the confidence and skill to do so. Be aware, though, that certain types of lettering lend themselves to carving: thin or curvy styles of lettering are much more difficult than clear block letters. Also, when you are starting out, the larger and chunkier the lettering, the easier it is to work with. Again, think about how much detail you are capable of rendering at this point in your crafting.

WHITTLING

While not completely necessary, clamping the project to your work surface does ensure that it won't slip around while you are carving the letters. Now that you have the letters stenciled or drawn, begin the carving: you can either decide to carve within the letter, making the letters embedded into the wood, or around the letter, making the letters stand out like a stamp (the latter is probably more difficult). You can use a basic whittling knife for the process, but if you have decided to dive into the whittling and woodworking hobby, then you might be advised to invest in a couple of additional tools, such as a small right angle chisel and a flat chisel. These help you not only to carve letters with more precision, but also to add elements to your other work with greater detail. The right angle chisel allows you to carve away from yourself up through the stenciled or drawn letters, while the flat chisel allows you to clean up the edges by paring away smaller pieces of wood, refining the lettering. Flat chisels make vertical cuts and straight edges easier. As you are carving out the letters, be sure not to go more than ¾ of its thickness or you may weaken the wood, making it prone to breaking or cracking. When you are finished with the carving process, sand any rough edges away and paint or seal as described in previous projects above.

This is also a good project in which you can practice using leftover scraps of wood: if you have a decent chunk of wood that isn't large enough to start another project on, practice stenciling and carving a single letter into it until you have the confidence to tackle a full project. Not only will this expand your skill set but it will also keep you developing hand strength and precision for bigger and better projects later.

Technically, the process described here is what is known as "chip carving," rather than whittling. However, the two terms and processes are very much interchangeable and have more to do with cultural associations than clear differentiations in materials, tools, and projects. The term whittling is often used in rural America to describe the process of creating objects with knives out of a single piece of wood, while chip carving describes the process of carving decorative patterns (including lettering) into flat blocks of wood, primarily popular in European folk art. In any event, it helps to know that both of these styles of carving share commonalities, and the same basic knives and wood types are used in both. Knowing how to work in both mediums also gives you more range and skill in applying your creativity to various projects. It is also useful to note that, since the terms are often used in similar circumstances, you can discover a wider range of projects to undertake by knowing both terms. Basically, as the woodworking site *Make It Wood* explains it, "The general view is that whittling is the act of carving wood while using only a straight-edged knife while wood carving involves using a wider assortment of tools to reach the desired outcome." Still, the debate is mainly one for purists and, again, the skills picked up via chip carving come in handy for any whittling project, turning beginning projects into expert pieces with finer detail.

Natural Designs

Creating a representation of something from nature using a natural product such as wood creates a special project, a convergence of natural materials and natural designs that serve to enhance the end product. This can be done in various ways, either via the relief carving that is discussed in the previous section, or via more classical techniques of whittling. These nature projects can be beautiful displays for your home or garden, as well as excellent practice for more ambitious ideas. For example, if you have really become excited about making your whittled animals as described in the first section in this chapter, you might want to start creating a habitat

WHITTLING

for them, replete with flowers and trees, leaves and other forest details. This is a wonderful way in which to think about all of your whittling projects: what will this small project contribute to a larger idea? Rather than conceive of each whittling project as a singular event – though, of course, it certainly can be – you can think of your whittling projects as part of a larger creative project. Just as with the train cars eventually making an entire train set, you can start to imagine how your various smaller projects can lead to something larger in scope.

In terms of natural designs, many whittlers focus on flowers and leaves because they are simultaneously made up of simple geometric shapes while containing the possibility for lots of specific and precise detail. That is to say that you can whittle a fairly simple flower out of a central circle, surrounded by ovals, attached to a rectangle, or you can carve an elaborately detailed flower with many petals, leaves, and customized elements. Start simple, then embellish as you get more comfortable with your skills. For a small starter project, try the following version which can be made from the smallest of scraps:

- Pick out a small branch or other long, slender piece of wood. If you are just starting out, you might want something that is a little sturdier; as you become more skilled, you can learn to whittle out of the thinnest twigs lying about.

WHITTLING

- If you are using a found branch, first take care to whittle off all of the outer bark (this will dry out once the project is complete and fall off).

- Using the tip of a very sharp small blade, carve a very thin piece of wood (almost a shaving) about ¼ to ⅓ of the way down the branch. Rotate slightly and repeat: these are the flower petals.

- Complete your rotation all around the twig until you have one layer of thinly shaved petals. If you are using a found twig or branch, this green wood will naturally curl a bit forming the shape of flower petals.

- Now, make an additional row or two of thinly shaved petals, either positioning them in between your previous petals or stopping right above the rows to make a fuller flower.

- Once you are done with your petals, remove the remaining central core of the twig that is above the petals.

- At this point, you probably want to whittle away at your stem so that it's thickness is in proportion to the flower petals you have created. It's not absolutely necessary, but use your judgment based on how you want your project to look.

- Using the same technique as with the flower petals above, shave two or three "leaves" below the petals to create a classic flower look.

- Trim the "stem" of the flower to whatever length you desire, then rearrange the petals and leaves as you like for the best appearance. Typically, these can be manipulated without breaking, though do use care.

- Now, you can paint your flower, if you like, or seal it with spray lacquer. You can also mount the flower on a bed of mulch or into a larger log or piece of wood for a natural base, or you can find artificial bases of Styrofoam and the like if you want. Essentially, just by using little found twigs or scraps of leftover wood, you can whittle a whole bed of flowers!

Other popular whittling projects that mimic natural objects are to tackle leaves or carve feather designs. Again, both of these objects are comprised of simple geometric shapes that can be rounded or varied depending on your skill level. A leaf can be as simple as a set of triangles around a central point with a small stem at the bottom and a light center line carved through the middle. A feather can be carved out a long rectangle by simply creating a top point and rounding the edges down to a shaft; the identifying marks of the feather can be as straightforward as making small diagonal cuts from each side toward the center. These are projects that make for

WHITTLING

good practice because they are quick and relatively easy. These are also good projects for painting, as this is the way to add depth and detail to simple projects while you are honing your skills. Look to the next section here for some advice on how to paint any number of your projects.

There are also food projects that whittlers take up, another small project that could lead to a large collection (think: a single carved wooden fruit leads to a full bowl of beautiful imitation fruits). If you refer back to the very first project mentioned in this chapter, the wooden egg, you already have the basic idea of how to create an orange or an apple or a pear with just a few modifications. Whittling a pineapple is also an exercise in following simple geometric patterns, and even the most rudimentary pineapple looks fun and unique in an imitation fruit bowl. You can also revisit that wooden egg for the Easter holidays for another example of a single object turned larger project: make a set of a dozen, paint them like classic Easter eggs and put them in a recycled egg carton as a lovely gift or centerpiece décor. As you become more experienced, you can learn to carve designs into the eggs, rather than relying on paint for variation. In the next chapter, there are some instructions for how to make more complicated patterns within an egg or cylinder shape.

Another popular food whittling project is the mushroom: first, it is also a rather simple design to model without a lot of measuring and marking; second, if you have conquered the wooden egg, then you are now well-versed in how to make the rounded shape of a mushroom cap. Finally, a little forest of mushrooms to go with your lawn gnome makes an even more unique lawn display. As with most of these whittling projects, you can customize as you go, either with whittling more detail or painting: for example, you can carve some spots on your mushroom cap, or you can simply paint them on. Look at various pictures of mushrooms, as well; there is nearly an infinite variety of shapes, sizes, and wild designs. The most basic supermarket mushroom is the model you want to use when beginning, but you can branch out to shiitakes, morels (with their intricate looping patterns; these take more time but aren't necessarily more complicated), or larger varieties such as maitakes and portobellos. In addition, if you get the hang of whittling a mushroom, then you are poised to make the transition to whittling other objects that have a similar pattern to them, such as trees which require more precision of detail.

Painted Projects

While it isn't necessary to paint your whittling projects (indeed, there are times when painting might actually obscure the quality of the work), there are many instances when painting might add interest, detail, and brightness to a finished product. There are other

WHITTLING

examples wherein painting is key to conveying what the finished product actually is (such as the fruit bowl mentioned in the previous section). In any case, painted projects give you another outlet for your creativity and skill to shine through your various projects. Learning how to apply and seal paint properly will ensure that your projects look their best and last through the years.

First, always prepare your wood before you paint it: while there are some purists who don't approve of sanding down a whittled project – that rustic look is part of the point – most of the time it's necessary for work that is to be painted. Sanding down the rough edges also gets rid of any splinters or splits in the wood which can eventually end up weakening the wood itself. When sanding, use 140 to 180-grit sandpaper, or use a sanding sponge (this works better on curvy surfaces and rounded

WHITTLING

ends). Remember to sand with the grain, not against it, which produces the smoothest and finest result. Also be sure to get rid of any residue, dust, or grit before you move on with your primer; a tack cloth works best for this, though a slightly damp rag will work in a pinch. Tack cloth can be found near the sandpaper in any good crafts section. Skipping this step can prevent the primer and/or paint from adhering to the surface, and it can certainly create clumps of paint or bare spots where debris has been left behind.

Second, while it isn't absolutely necessary to use primer, it is almost always a very good idea to do so, especially if you are creating objects (such as toys for children to pass on to their children) intended to last a lifetime. You can either spray or paint the primer on, depending on your preference and the size of the object; be aware when using spray to get it into the crevices and such. Primer not only helps the paint to adhere to the wood, but it can also make the end result seem brighter and fresher. It is particularly noticeable when you are using light-colored paints. Without the primer, those lighter colors might look faded or dull. When priming, cover the front and sides first, and let that dry before applying a coat to the back and base. Some experts recommend that you then sand your wood again, applying a second coat of primer after that: this leads to an exceptionally smooth and bright finish. This additional step is, of course, up to your discretion, depending on what you intend for the final look as well as how much time you have to complete it. Always be sure that the primer is completely dry before moving on to the next step.

Now, you are at last ready to paint: acrylic paint is typically the paint of choice for crafters working with wood; it's vibrant, relatively easy to work with, and it dries quickly. Oil paints can be used but they are less forgiving and usually more expensive. Crafting paint usually comes in small plastic bottles, though you can find artist-grade acrylic paint (of slightly higher quality) in tubes; this artist-grade paint usually needs to be thinned a bit with water before using. In any case, it's wise to use some kind of palette or small, disposable containers to paint from, rather than painting directly from the bottle. However, because acrylic does dry quickly, be sure not to pour too much out at once.

When choosing brushes, avoid super-stiff brushes (which will leave visible strokes and are harder to manipulate into small spaces); instead, look for sable or Taklon brushes. Also, beware of overloading your brush with paint to avoid globs and drips; the paint should only come up about halfway on the bristles. Always keep a cup of water handy, even if you are only using one color at a time; dip the brush often in the water to keep it supple and ready to go. Of course, when switching between colors, be sure to wash off the previous color well before moving on.

WHITTLING

Before you begin the painting process, it is also important to have a plan for what, where, and how you plan to paint your wood: depending on the project, you may want to apply a base coat over the entire object before adding details; in that case, apply your base paint, let it dry thoroughly, and then apply another. In most cases, however, you will probably just be painting particular details on your project; again, start with the front and sides, let that dry completely, then move to the back and base. Making sure that paint is thoroughly dry before adding more paint or detail, or finishing with sealer, is important; even though it might look dry or feel dry to the touch, that does not mean that it's fully dry. Look at the instructions on the brand of paint you've purchased, which should have some basic guidelines. If you don't find those, give your project a 24-hour window in which to dry, just to be safe.

Finally, finish off your project with sealer, either spray-on or brush-on. Choose the sealer that you feel will enhance the look and style of your project the best: there is matte, which does not add additional shine; glossy, which does add additional shine; and satin, which is somewhere in between. After you apply the first coat, let it dry thoroughly and decide whether it needs a second. Of course, anytime you are painting and sealing, be sure to do so in a well-ventilated area to prevent illness or injury.

WHITTLING

Aside from colored paint, you always have the option either to seal the finished product with any of the varieties of sealer mentioned above or to apply a stain to the wood, which will enhance the grain and deepen the color. However you decide to finish your wooden masterpieces, applying at least some of these processes will enliven your project and keep it vibrant and strong for years to come.

Survival Skills

Another category of projects for the whittler is that which accompanies an outdoorsy approach to life. Indeed, the stereotypical whittler is someone who spends time outdoors, camping and fishing and the like; this is where all that found wood comes from! Thus, it makes sense that a lot of whittling projects are in some way connected to those outdoor activities. Many of these projects are highly practical and very useful for spending time out in nature.

For example, if you know how to handle a knife well, then you can quickly and easily carve out your own tent stakes for camping. This is a skill that undeniably comes in handy if you spend a lot of time in tents; losing or breaking a tent stake can spell disaster if you don't have a back-up. This is a kind of supersized "whittling" that will serve you well when out in the woods. Basically, all you need is a good knife (some experts recommend a serrated knife for this kind of large-scale, small-detail job) and a decent-sized piece of wood. Find something that is at least one or two inches in diameter, about a foot in length, and make sure that your branch isn't rotted out or weakened in some way before you begin; if the wood sounds hollow when you tap it, that could be an indication that it is rotten on the inside. Once you've gotten your branch chosen or cut to size, carve a notch in it about one and a half inches up from what will the top (blunt) end. This is to help secure your cord to the stake. Next, sharpen the other end of the stick, making a clearly defined point of about one to two inches in length; the more defined the point, the easier it will be to drive it into the ground. This is one of the simplest and most practical projects you can learn.

There are other practical applications to whittling, as well. A lot of outdoorsmen and women like to know how to carve their own wooden knife or machete-like instrument. Mostly, this project is just for fun or practice, but there is some practical application in having a wooden knife; it can be used to clear pathways of brush or low-hanging branches or assist in rudimentary cooking tasks. In any event, making a wooden knife is almost as simple as making a tent stake:

- First, choose the appropriate length of strong wood for your project, a little longer than what you want your final product to be. Again, make sure the wood isn't rotted. Of course, it would also be wise to pick out a piece of wood that is already somewhat flat rather than round.

- Next, delineate the handle from the blade by making a clear stop cut around the entire piece, then shave down to the tip of the knife, forming your sharpened "blade" and defining the tip.

- Once you have the knife defined and sharpened as you like, sand it down (again, sanding with the grain) in order to both smooth out the roughness and to further sharpen the wooden blade.

- Return to your handle and clean that up, if necessary, or add decorative notes, if you like. Then, to make a handle that is easy to grip and comfortable in the hand, wrap twine or other durable material around the handle, securing it with wood glue or superglue.

In addition to knives, many whittlers and woodworkers enjoy making other utensils with their hobby. One of the most popular is the wooden spoon and spatula; these kinds of well-crafted wooden utensils are sought out by avid home cooks – they feel better in the hand than plastic, taking on a lovely patina over time, and they don't scratch the surfaces of pans and casserole dishes. Of course, lots of home cooks also seek out wooden bowls and platters, though these are somewhat

WHITTLING

beyond the purview of basic whittling, usually requiring lathes or other mechanical tools.

Wooden spoons, on the other hand, are simple to make and beautiful to behold. You can find any number of wooden spoon making kits, of course, which come with a basic knife, a hook knife (for rounding the bowl of the spoon), and a chip carver, as well as a sharpening strop and a polishing compound for finishing the spoon. However, you can, with a little practice, whittle a wooden spoon from the most basic of materials. This is another great project for picking up some practice and building hand strength.

WHITTLING

Finally, another fun and useful project that the outdoorsy whittler can try their hand at is a wooden fishing lure; not only might it actually work as a lure with the addition of some hooks, but it also makes a lovely folk gift for the avid fisherman or woman. You can simply trace the fish design on your wood and carve out a basic fish shape, then add some detail like gills and eyes once you have your roughed-out fish. For extra pizzazz, you can, of course, paint the fish, but you can also add some additional detail if it is to be a display project. For example, using thin copper sheets to make fins will give it some shine and interest or you can attach your lure to some kind of stand with fishing line or other gear so that it can be easily displayed.

WHITTLING

Art for Art's Sake

Finally, whittling isn't necessarily about creating objects for practical use or for entertainment, as it can also be a hobby that provides an outlet for creative and artistic expression. Even though whittling is often derided as mere "folk art" – which is typically used as a dismissive phrase in sophisticated art circles – its products can quite clearly become something more meaningful and beautiful to their creator. That is, even though we might stereotypically think of whittling as an old man's rural pastime, this kind of woodworking craftsmanship can legitimately be a higher form of art. In fact, over the last couple of decades, the art world has begun to recognize traditional crafting projects and other kinds of folk art as legitimate artistic endeavors. Indeed, the Art Institute of Chicago mounted a display of what they termed "tramp art" of beautiful wooden objects likely made by transient workers or those drawn to the sprawl of American life on the open road. In addition, new found respect for the beauty in objects that have been created by people in rural communities across the country, as well as across the world, has burgeoned in recent years. In general, folk art expresses the traditions and aspirations of a particular culture, whether it be an object of utility or of decoration.

Thus, should you become immersed in your new-found hobby, you will find that there are lots of opportunities for artistic expression – art for art's sake

– that will take you to new creative heights. Clearly, these kinds of projects allow you the freedom to dream up whatever kind of project appeals to you, and they can provide you with a platform to express a feeling, an idea, an objection, or a message that you believe has meaning.

For example, one of the consistent features in a lot of woodworking (and metalworking) projects has been the use of Celtic symbols and design elements. There is a lot of reclamation of a distant past, as well as tributes to the far-away worlds and cultures that these symbols and designs evoke. So, you can make a wooden spoon – practical, useful – and carve a Celtic design into the handle – beautiful, even meaningful – into an artistic object or you might be inspired to whittle something purely decorative, a wooden Celtic symbol that can be worn as a pendant. The appeal of the Celtic design is likely in its geometric patterns, which are conducive to basic woodworking and metalworking as well as inherently beautiful in its intricate configurations. These symbols also carry with them meanings and connections to history that are appealing to many.

WHITTLING

Another artistic endeavor associated with folk art from a particular culture is the history of totems within Native American or other indigenous groups. These symbolic objects are layered with history, with culture, with meaning – and imbued with beauty, artistic expertise, and sometimes political expression. Making a totem pole was about telling the story of a particular group in a creative and artistic manner with materials that were readily available. This is an example of how the general practice of woodworking is embedded within particular cultural traditions and, as such, is something greater than it might first appear. As well, the Native Americans certainly weren't the only people who recognized the power of totems as storytelling objects: you can find Trajan's Column made of marble in Rome, telling the story of the emperor's campaigns and successes. In this manner, your whittling hobby can transcend its form, telling a specific story about a particular time – even making a train set, one car at a time, for a child to cherish and pass on is a personal version of this kind of artistic storytelling.

Even if you aren't interested in exploring particular cultural expressions of folk art, you still have a whole host of potential projects that are simply beautiful or stirring objects for their own sake. Looking through some examples online, you can find projects that are tributes to South Pacific culture, the clean lines and distinctive geometric patterns that evoke Tiki-style objects; you can also find whittled Moai faces, the emblematic and enigmatic statues that ring the far-flung Easter Islands; there are also numerous projects that evoke the "spirit" of the wood, paying homage to nature and its resources. Essentially, if you begin to see your hobby as a way in which to channel your creativity and to create beauty, there are no limitations to what you can produce besides learning, practicing, and honing your skills. Start by taking some chances with leftover scraps, and you may just find your inner artist.

WHITTLING

Chapter Summary

Embarking on some simple projects will hone your whittling skills, while giving you the opportunity to create gifts, unique decor, and even useful items for yourself, your family, and your friends.

- Start by making a wooden egg, which will help build hand strength and teach you how to work with wood grain.

- Remember in the beginning to focus on simple geometric shapes and abstract representations as you develop your abilities.

- Also, break down projects into manageable pieces; this is key to creating a successful end product and avoiding frustration.

- Note that whittling can be a meaningful form of creative and artistic expression.

In the next chapter, you will learn some more advanced whittling projects than those we've just covered. These projects will most likely take you longer, possibly several days, and they'll require you to demonstrate all of the cuts and techniques that we've covered throughout the book thus far.

CHAPTER FIVE

ADVANCED PROJECTS

After practicing with a number of beginning projects, you can now begin to expand your skill set by working on some more advanced projects. The craft of whittling itself leads into more complicated projects and more expert ways of woodworking in general. In this chapter, you will find a whole host of ideas for more advanced projects, along with some additional suggestions about how to parlay your craft into long-lasting delights for friends and family alike. Finding a creative outlet, especially when the world undergoes changes and troubles, will give you a way to channel your energy into productive and pleasing projects.

Of course, as you transition into more advanced projects, you may decide you want to invest in more knives – as has already been suggested in the previous chapter for certain projects – or more tools in general. Once you decide that this hobby is one that you want to stick with, then you can make a fair decision on whether to invest in more tools. Whittling itself is kind of a gateway hobby to more advanced forms of woodworking in general, and you may find that, in order to fully realize your creative designs and complex projects, you might move beyond the simplicity of a single knife and a block of wood that is inherent to whittling. Having said that, there is still yet something deeply satisfying in sticking to simplicity and trying to elevate the complexity of your projects.

Animal Animations

Now that you have had some practice in whittling, you can return to certain beginning projects with more expertise and, perhaps, enthusiasm. Instead of imagining the abstract and basic shapes of various animals, you are equipped to whittle out more representative figures with more detail and exactness. The simple geometric shapes of the cat and the rabbit, all rounds and ovals and triangles, can give way to the more complicated and sinuous forms as the elephant, with its winding trunk, or a glorious bird, with resplendent feathers and spiky talons. Basically, once you learn how to whittle away the simple shapes, your eye will grow keener and your hand will grow surer about how to engage in more complex shapes. One basic rule of thumb to keep in mind, however, is to start with a drawing, either of your own rendering or from some clear-eyed source; trace it onto

WHITTLING

your block of wood before you get started, and mark out the gradations from one piece or body part to the other, making measurements when necessary for perspective and balance to be maintained.

Also, when you start to think of more advanced projects, your mind might immediately leap to bigger and bolder projects – and certainly, that can be the case – but improving your abilities as a woodworker often has to do with being able to wrest detail out of the smaller pieces. To that end, try your hand at the following: this uses just a branch to form a fish leaping out of splashing water, both simple in its elegance and complex in its detail.

- Start by tracking down a nice, sturdy branch that is two or three inches in diameter, preferably with a nub of a branch shooting off to one side; this will be for the dorsal fin of your fish.

- Then, remove the bark from the entire branch, and sketch your fish onto the denuded branch (sketch it out on paper first, to be confident, if you like).

- The sketch can be fairly simple, at this point: a rounded head topped by a dorsal fin and a gaping mouth as if the fish is about to latch onto a lure. Whittle around your rough sketch at the front, then taper the dorsal fin to your liking.

WHITTLING

- Don't worry about the back of the body, the tail and such, as you are going to whittle this part into water for the fish to be leaping out of.

- Make sure your basic fish is shaped to your liking, then sand it down entirely; this will help you with making the splashing water.

- With the sharpest point of your blade, pull cut little shavings down away from the fish to make curls of waves. Do this all the way around, making the shavings of various lengths to showcase the splash.

- Now, add the side fins to the fish by making shallow, gentle cuts and fanning them out just a bit so they look like three-dimensional fins.

- At this point, you can add more detail, such as eyes and cross-hatch scales. When you are finished, seal or paint as desired.

Fish, of course, have a special place in the annals of whittling projects, attractive to the outdoorsy types who are likely to practice this folk art. And, you can see marvelous examples of extraordinarily detailed fish carvings, as well as all sorts of examples of other projects, on the internet. Use your imagination and your skill as a guide to what you can accomplish. Return to your earliest projects on animals, such as the simple cat or dog abstraction, and redraw those projects with more realistic detail, such as trying to render eyes or even carve

WHITTLING

fur. Think of the animators at Pixar: the original *Toy Story* was successful in creating objects that were made of plastic and wood, but it wasn't very good at rendering humans very realistically. However, as the animators have gotten better at their craft – and the technology available to them has improved – the realism of later installations in the series, as well as in other Pixar movies, is apparent. This is the kind of leap that you are aiming for, from the beginner's craft of making abstractions to the advanced turn of aiming for realism.

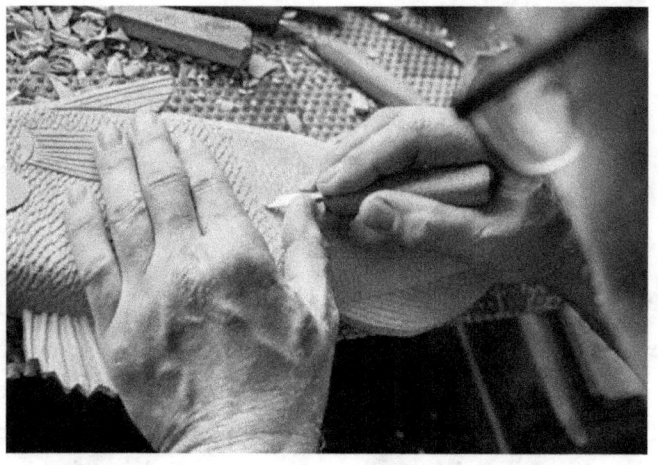

Flights of Fancy

Having discussed realism above, we turn our attention back to fanciful creations that you can create now that you have more practice under your belt. This

WHITTLING

doesn't mean that you abandon "realism" of expression; it just means that there is just as much fun to have by creating magical creatures and fantastical designs that require more skill and a greater level of detail.

For example, in the beginner's chapter, you learned how to create a wizard face, which is a fairly simple process of marking out basic shapes. Now, turn your attention to carving a full-bodied wizard (or Yoda, our other example from the previous chapter). This will require attention to proportion, specificity in measurement, and a more refined set of details. Instead of just a face with a beard topped by a hat, you can turn your attention also to a flowing set of robes, distinctive arms, and perhaps a staff topped with an orb – these things always signify "wizard!" There are some basic tips for how to designate proportion for humanoid figures:

- To follow the rules of classical sculpture, you designate the "8HU" method, which means the 8-head unit of measuring, wherein the head is about ⅛ the proportion of the total body. This actually makes the head a bit larger than is totally realistic (like Michelangelo's David, for example), but works well if you want to implement a grandeur to your carving.

- To follow the more realistic rule in human proportions, you would have a head that is about 6.5 or 7.5 of the total body. This, of course, is more difficult in terms of measuring, but there are calculators available online to help you determine, in centimeters, how much 6.5 or 7.5 of the length you have to carve is.

- Also, basic human proportions designate that about ½ the length of the carving be from the head to the crotch area, at the bottom of the pelvis, with the other ½ being from there to the feet. Thus, if you are carving a two-foot length of wood, one foot is for the top half of the body and so on, while the head would be about three inches, according to the classical proportions.

- The upper and lower halves of the body are not directly proportional, of course, with the distance between the neck and pectoral area shorter than the distance between the pectoral area and the belly button. Use a proportional calculator or your best judgment in marking the measurements out. This gives you a basic starting point.

Of course, if you are carving something like a Yoda figure (or any kind of muppet-type figure), the head will be proportionally larger than the body and, thus, potentially simpler than a realistic human figure. Nevertheless, in any case, once you start to whittle whole figures, the necessity of measuring out and marking your proportions becomes more important to the success of your final project.

WHITTLING

There are other fantastical figures that seem to attract those who work with wood: dragons, of course, are frequently found alongside elves and dwarves and other creatures that populate the landscape of famous fantasy franchises such as *Lord of the Rings* and *Game of Thrones*. These more intricate projects have the advantage of currently remaining hugely popular, so you can find lots of examples and some lengthy step-by-step videos on how to produce them. But you can also draw your own example and work from there, following the same logic as introduced in the previous chapter: start with the head – a dragon's head offers a great deal of detail right off the bat – and work your way up to the entire body. Again, think in parts, from the head to the wings to the body to the tail. In fact, you could, if you aren't worried about being a complete purist, conceivably carve each piece to your liking, then put them together in the end. While this strays a bit from the common definition of whittling – one knife to one piece of wood – it may ultimately satisfy your creative desires while you learn more about the process. Consider this a longer-term project, perfecting each part, before learning how to proportion them into a viable full-bodied creature, and finally trying your hand at whittling a full dragon out of one block of wood.

Other popular fantasy figures include the ubiquitous gnome, of course, along with elves and fairies, gargoyles and unicorns. You could arguably make a menagerie of fantasy characters either for display or for play, as with the toys that we return to below.

Games Galore

Revisiting your toy making projects, here you can start to think outside of the creative box. Of course, when making toys for small children, the most important issue to consider is the safety of the toy (hence, why sanding is important, as well as paying attention to potential choking hazards). Within those parameters, though, there is a lot that can be dreamed up: for example, taking the long view of the train set project, your cars can get more and more elaborate as you go, employing new skills and greater detail as you practice.

You can also consider creating toys with actual moving parts. Again, this might move slightly beyond the purist definition of whittling, but it is an extension of the craft that brings with it interesting challenges and delightful payoffs. Think about the train set as a template: making an actual car is akin to making a basic boxcar, but you can add actual wheels that turn for a more kinesthetic product. This can lead to any number of trucks, cars, and other moving vehicles should you have a youngster who is invested in these types of toys. You can also consider articulated toys, such as puppets, or interactive toys that require gears; all of these items can be made from wood, though they require assembly and some basic engineering skills. In addition, think of

WHITTLING

the longer-term payoff: not only will you be producing one-of-a-kind objects that will delight your children, grandchildren, or others, but you might also be instilling in them a desire to work with wood as their own creative outlet. Just as children who are read books when they are young often grow up to be readers, children who play with these wooden toys often grow up to harbor a nostalgia about them. Thus, you are potentially fostering a generational tradition.

Why not also consider embarking on a wooden toy chest in which those toys can be kept and preserved? Again, this likely will move you beyond the simple craft of whittling, but it employs many of the same skills but with different challenges. Even if you don't have the tools or time to embark on such a large project, you probably want to provide something of equal durability and beauty in which to store the toys you painstakingly make. Toy boxes seem almost like quaint relics of a pre-technological past, yet they are quite practical and can also be quite whimsical or beautiful.

To return to whittling in its purer form, you can also revisit the idea of making chess pieces, as discussed in the beginner's section, and think of more elaborate ways in which you can customize a particular set. For example, as mentioned in the previous section, *Game of Thrones* was one of the most successful television series of all time and retains loyal fans: think of carving a set based on the characters in the series (though you'd have to decide who, ultimately, should be king) – there are clearly many candidates for who might be pawns, of course, and certainly some castles upon which to model your pieces. If fantasy is not your style, then consider carving a classical set with its more difficult curves and greater detail, or riffing on your own favorite franchise (*Star Wars* set, for example, or how about an *Avengers* theme?). Again, this is an extension of what you have attempted when starting out.

Finally, all toys are subject to lots and lots of handling – whether it be from little ones who are prone to putting pieces in their mouths or dragging them through dirt and mud and everything in between to adults playing with a homemade chess set, touching each piece regularly – and thus need some consistent upkeep in order to maintain cleanliness, repair cracks or another injury, and restore beauty. Wood products are especially prone to collecting grease which impacts the amount of dirt and dust they also pick up, so maintain cleanliness by wiping down toys (ideally after each use) with a clean cloth and some mild wood cleanser. Be sure to target areas such as crevices that collect more grime or handles that are constantly touched. If a toy is damaged in a mild way, such as a little ding or scratch, it can usually be repaired by using a filler wax crayon that matches the color of the object; if the damage is more noticeable, you might need to sand it down a bit and restain or repaint. In either case, the more quickly you repair the damage after it has been done, the more likely you will get a result that is closest to the original. Finally, if you store them well and care for them regularly, you can extend the life of these toys almost indefinitely.

Holiday Hobbies

One of the best times of the year for you to expand your repertoire of projects is at the holidays: these give you a theme on which to focus, as well as a growing collection of decorations or gifts that are wholly unique. These times of the year also serve as reminders of how much progress you have made in improving your abilities and honing your craft.

Start with the New Year's holiday: think about carving numbers to spell out the New Year, each number from a single block of wood. This moves you beyond simple relief carving into shaping and rounding the numbers, using some of the skills you developed with the wooden egg exercise. You could also consider making a yearly calendar, the perpetual wooden calendars that you can find in craft stores; this means making some sort of base for the wooden blocks that mark the month and day in them. There are several different styles of how to set this up; they can easily be perused online. This would not only make a marvelous gift, it is also a practical and renewable resource that will last throughout the years.

WHITTLING

For Valentine's Day, you could pursue the interlocking hearts carving, a popular challenge for advanced woodworkers: start with a block of wood that you carve into a thick cross, then turn that cross into two interlocking squares. Next, sketch the hearts directly onto the squares, so that you have a clear pattern to follow. Cut away at your design until you clearly have two heart shapes; the hardest part is separating them, which essentially means cutting away the centers of the hearts, leaving the outline of the hearts intertwined with one another. This may take some practice and some visual aids (there are many available online), but it is a challenging project that can still be completed in a relatively short amount of time. When you are done, sand down the pieces and paint, stain, or seal as you like.

For the Fourth of July, try your hand at something different – and more ephemeral – to elevate your backyard celebration: turn your new-found carving skills to a watermelon, and carve up a watermelon to resemble the American flag or a fireworks display. While this isn't

WHITTLING

whittling, per se, it is a lovely way to show off your skills in a manner that is both impressive and edible. Your family and guests will be happy to help you finish it off!

There are other projects you could undertake for the spring or fall months: the ideas for Easter or Passover or the spring equinox run the gamut from animal figurines to eggs to crosses to floral patterns. You can also think about wooden turkeys or cornucopias for Thanksgiving: the cornucopia (horn of plenty), in particular, will give you a whole host of individual projects to create within the larger idea. Imagine a curved horn (one piece), out of which spills a whole host of foodstuffs (grapes and apples, pears and pumpkins) and nature's bounty (flowers and leaves and vines). See below, in Natural Designs, for a step by step guide to carving a leaf.

Finally, there is always something fun about creating more decorations for Christmas, and now that you have more confidence in your skills, try for something that is more animated than your previous attempts. Here is a set of basic instructions for how to create a whistle in the shape of Santa:

- The only special equipment you will need here is a drill for the whistle hole.

- Find a branch that's about five or six inches long with a diameter of about an inch.

WHITTLING

- Make your whistle first: drill a hole in the center of one end of the branch, making it about ¾ of an inch in diameter and about two inches deep. The sound of the whistle is determined by how deep the hole is; the sound becomes deeper as the hole itself is deeper.

- Next, carve out your mouthpiece by making an angled cut about ½ inch down from the hole you've drilled on each side. Round out and sand the cut so that it is comfortable to the mouth.

- For a more advanced whistle, with a range of sound, you can drill holes at the bottom of the whistle (as in a flute).

- Define the area that you want to carve your Santa face in; the face should be visible to viewers as you use the whistle. Outline the area and make a stop cut around it.

- Now mark a centerline, then angle the knife up toward the centerline to make the bridge of the nose.

- Draw on your eyes, and then carve out the eye sockets (don't go too deeply) and define the nose.

- Define your mouth with deep smile lines, then make a stop cut here and cut out a small triangle (the mouth itself).

WHITTLING

- Next, mark the lines for the mustache and beard, and carve these out; depending on how you want your finished Santa to look (and your skill level), you can create waves and curls in the long beard.

- Finally, go back and carve out the eyes, making wrinkles as your preference and skill dictate.

- Here you can also add other details, as you like, such as a set of bushy eyebrows or a Santa hat, if you have the space.

- Gently sand your finished piece and paint it, if you like. The paint will give you the final touches, making the figure clearly identifiable as a Santa figure.

Don't forget, also, the opportunities for taking your skills to the next level with your holiday projects: you could carve the base or stand for a small tree with Santa's workshop designs, for example, or make a North Pole pointer sign for your yard. Again, some of these larger projects would probably require more than a pocket knife, of course, but the skills you apply will be quite similar.

WHITTLING

Home and Garden Décor

Home projects for the advanced whittler can become anything from practical to elaborate. For example, once you have the knack of making a wooden spoon and/or spatula, as discussed in the previous chapter, you might want to tackle more utensils, making a set for the kitchen or as gifts for friends. At this point, you should be able to add designs, like the Celtic knot (which is popular on wooden spoons) or a floral pattern, or other personalized touches. Think about Laguiole brand knives: the distinctive bumblebee atop the tang at the handle immediately identifies the product as theirs (it originated with Napoleon himself). You can come up with your own identifying flourish if you like. You can also move beyond utensils to servingware, such as platters, mugs, and even bowls.

WHITTLING

One of the most treasured and lasting projects for the serious whittler is the *kuksa* mug. Also known as *Kasa*, *Guksi*, or *Noggin*, this wooden mug has been a mainstay among outdoorsmen and women for centuries. The *kuksa* tradition comes out of Scandinavia, and its beautiful design and hearty structure just begs for a warm beverage to hold during a cold winter's night. This is truly a keepsake for the ages and an advanced project to make any whittler proud.

- It is worth your while to do some research on traditional *kuksa* cups and designs, figuring out which would most fit your style and skill set, before you begin.

- Also, be sure to make numerous drawings of your cup before you begin, trying it out at different angles, solving problems before they arise is one way to get the most out of your block of wood.

- Select wood for this kind of project carefully: wood with grain that's too open isn't ideal for holding liquids, of course. Most expert carvers recommend birch for the *kuksa* cup, and more specifically, they recommend a birch burl, which will automatically provide you with a rounded shape on which to model your cup.

- Once you have your burl roughed out (which you can either do with an ax yourself or trust to

WHITTLING

a woodworking shop), you can begin to carve with the grain and along the natural curve of the burl. You want the shape to follow the organic pattern of the wood as much as possible, as this produces a stronger final product.

- Whittle away until you have your cup defined, with the lip and the handle formed enough. This is easier to do with green wood, of course, and be sure to keep your wood wet as you work (if you have to stay away from the project for a day or two, wrap it well in plastic to keep it somewhat moist).

- Once you have the basic shape of the cup complete, start to hollow out the bowl; wait until that is done before you finish up the outside. This is where you must be careful not to crack the wood. Keeping the wood moist is one key to preventing cracks, as well as working quickly so the thinner layers don't dry unevenly. You want the outside shape of the cup and the inside hollow to dry at the same rate, if possible. A spoon knife will help this process along.

- Now, make sure your *kuksa* cup is thoroughly dry before sanding and finishing: this must be done slowly in order to ensure a sturdy cup that won't crack. One method for drying your cup slowly is to put it in a resealable plastic bag with the seal only partially open; put it in a cool, dry

WHITTLING

place and wait until you see beads of moisture form on the bag. Turn the bag inside-out, replace the cup inside and let it dry again until you see no droplets on the bag. Check it frequently during this process as you don't want mold to grow on your wood.

- Wait another week, placing your cup in a cool, dry place for further drying.

- After the cup is completely dry, use a freshly sharpened knife to smooth out the rough cuts; this will save time and energy in sanding. Then, work on sanding starting with an 80 grit and working your way up to 800 or 1200 grit, depending on how smooth and durable you want the final product to be. Don't skip any grits in between for best results. The first sanding will require the most work, of course, and subsequent sandings will bring more beauty and durability to the finish.

- Most traditional *kuksa* cups have some sort of embellishment on them that make the product truly unique. Draw your design carefully before transferring it to the handle or side or bottom of the cup. Use good quality acrylic paints to make your personal carving stand out.

- Finally, finish the cup with food-safe hardening oil: be sure to coat thoroughly, letting it absorb the oil until it cannot take in any more, and let it dry upside down touching as little surface as possible. You are not oiling the bowl of the cup, as it will affect the taste of anything you drink out of it – just the outside. Give it a couple of weeks to cure thoroughly.

- Before using it for the first time, fill the *kuksa* with hot water and rinse a few times, just to get rid of any potential off flavors.

Don't forget about lawn and garden projects, as well: you can put your advanced whittling skills to work on creating personalized fence designs, for example, giving your backyard some personal flair. If you have a vegetable or herb garden, you can whittle whimsical signs to indicate which plot grows which vegetables and herbs, rather than use the unattractive plastic labels that

WHITTLING

come with seeds or starter plants. You can also make a sign for the garden, of course.

You might also consider carving a cheery welcome sign for your home in general. This is a fairly straightforward project with lots of different styles from which to choose. For example, if you find a plank of wood about four or five inches wide and a couple of feet long, you could whittle out a WELCOME message vertically, with a personalized design at the top or around the borders. With a drill, you can easily make the sign ready to hang from a peg or with a wire loop. Again, think of something that might represent you and your family that welcomes people through your front door. There are various patterns available online that you could use as a jumping-off point if you like.

Interlocking Leisures

Aside from the aforementioned idea about the Welcome sign for your home, there are other lettering projects you might want to undertake now that you have improved your skill set. There are some common projects that many whittlers tackle both to challenge and hone their skill sets. These purely decorative projects help to expand your engineering talents, such as they are necessary to envision these projects while allowing you a space in which to practice more intricate tasks. The popular "ball in a cage" and "chain link" projects are two such projects that test the skills of the advanced whittler.

WHITTLING

- For the ball in a cage, you will need a small block of softwood, about 1" by 1" by 4" in length.

- Define your cage by marking lines ¼" from each corner, then ½" from each end. Finally, separate the three balls by marking an inch and a quarter from each end.

- Now that you have all of your lines marked, make stop cuts around the cage and the edges of the balls, not going too deep yet. Then, carve out triangular bits from each end of the cage to start defining the balls. Do the same carving in between the balls. Repeat this on all sides, and you will now have a rough outline of the balls inside the cage.

- Next, continue to carve out the balls, freeing them from each other and from the cage (though be careful not to cut the balls too small, or they will fall out of the cage). Smooth and round out the shapes as you go.

- Finish out the cage by smoothing out the edges, tapering at the top, if you like, for a more finished look. You now have something akin to a trompe l'oeil (trick of the eye): the balls can move about slightly in their cage but not be free of it; it looks as if you have done the impossible by imprisoning balls in a cage that are too large either to be inserted or released.

WHITTLING

Now, you can try your hand at a wooden "chain link" project, which can also be combined with the above project for a truly tricky looking final product.

- Start with the same size block as above (1" x 1" x 4"), and mark ¼" in from each side, then cut along those lines in order to carve out a rough cross shape.

- Now, mark the centers of the cross shape on ends opposite one another, then make another two marks 1" up from sides that have not yet been marked: this defines your three chain links, each about 2" long.

- Cut a v-shaped mark from the center line on each end, all the way to the flat of the cross; this defines your two links at each end. Then, make another v-shaped cut at the 1" mark from each side to form the middle link.

- Hollow out the end links and cut enough between them to separate. Follow your cuts toward the center link, shaping the end links as you go before hollowing out the center link.

- Smooth the finished cuts, as you like, and finish with lacquer or paint. Again, you have created something that looks rather impossible: three freely moving links that cannot be broken.

WHITTLING

Should you wish, you can even combine these projects into one continuous trompe l'oeil figure: basically, use a longer block of wood (about 12") in order to carve three links at one end, connecting to balls in a cage carving and ending with another three links. You can even carve a hook at one end for easy display. This is just one of the variations that you can create once you get accustomed to the process of linking and creating "moving" parts out of a single block of wood. Think about incorporating some of your own distinctive designs as you are making a linking chain, for example, or consider how the chain itself can be utilized to display other objects. These projects are excellent experiments to see how far you can develop these tricky and delightful little objects.

Natural Designs

Returning to nature for inspiration, you can now move beyond the basics of geometric patterns into detailed representations of natural objects. As suggested back in the beginner's section, as you start to become more skilled at creating whittled objects, you can move further into realistic depictions of your model subjects. Again, natural objects are sometimes fairly simple to whittle, as their basic components are geometric shapes; however, the more realistically you wish to depict something, the further you move away from that basic geometry. For example, carving an object that represents

WHITTLING

a tree is fairly straightforward: at its most basic, this could simply be carving out lines of different lengths and varying heft (a thick, long rectangle for a trunk with shorter and skinnier rectangles sprouting from the top of the main trunk gives you an abstract representation of a tree). Once you become more skilled, however, you can begin to work on the intricacies of what individual trees look like; instead of an abstract tree, you can try your hand at depicting a solid oak tree or a spindly birch or (perhaps most challenging) a shaggy willow tree. You are starting at the same basic point but using more detail and definition to move into a more realistic depiction. The first higher level of skill would be to make the tree more three-dimensional – instead of a flat cutout style of abstraction, you would make a rounded tree trunk atop which the branches are fleshed out. This, of course, requires a larger block of wood and a greater investment of time, but the results are magnificent. Remember, as well, that the key to making any project, whether simple or complex, is to sketch out your ideas first, then transfer them to your block before beginning. This works for all sorts of natural designs, such as the elaborate feather carving pictured below, as well as the leaf instructions that follow.

WHITTLING

If you aren't quite up to carving out an entire tree, then you can focus on a single leaf to start. Again, you are using the basic principles of geometry to get you started, but expanding in terms of detail and definition. Try this project for carving a realistic-looking leaf:

- Pick out an actual leaf to use for your project, something that is well-defined enough for you to work with in detail. For example, maple and oak leafs both have distinctive patterns.

- Now, trace the actual leaf onto your block of wood, making sure that the grain goes vertically from top to bottom which will help you in the carving process. It's probably a good idea not to choose a block that is too thick; that will take a lot of time to whittle it down to a manageable thickness.

WHITTLING

- Start carving out the basic outline of your leaf, whittling around your markings until you have the shape defined.

- Now, begin to refine the basic shape by rounding out certain edges and sharpening others, depending on your leaf and your vision for the final project.

- Once you have a realistic example of a leaf, then you can start to add specific detail to it: add veins and other fine details into the surface of your leaf, looking to your original specimen for guidance if you like. You can also whittle away at some of the leaf's edges to make the leaves look as if they are curling a bit. If you want a fall or winter leaf, you can even carve notches of decay into your leaf. This is all up to what you desire out of your final project.

- Finish your leaf by sanding it, if you like, and by painting and/or sealing it.

As with the tree project described above, this leaf can be part of a larger project: if you make several of these, they can be used as a harvest or Thanksgiving display; they could be part of a larger natural scene that you wish to create, complete with animal figures and other plant life; they could even become part of a larger tree itself (though this would truly be a monumental

WHITTLING

undertaking). Again, the artistic vision is derived from your expectations.

Other natural objects that can be carved, as we discussed in the previous chapter, are food items. Carving out a wooden fruit bowl is a fun beginner's project if you have the time and inclination. For a more advanced project, you might consider using your whittling skills on food itself: there is a long and illustrious tradition, particularly in some Asian cultures, of carving intricate designs and natural scenes onto actual pieces of food. These intricate creations – miles above your basic radish flower – have been revered for centuries, and they have recently spawned an entire category of viral videos and pictures of food items looking like non-food items and vice versa, or certain foods masquerading as other foods – like an ice cream "hamburger." (This is another example of the trompe l'oeil tradition, of "tricking the eye" into seeing something that isn't there or is something entirely different.) Think about how you can use your whittling skills to create something whimsical and beautiful out of a piece of food, then transfer that to a block of wood for something more permanent. There are numerous examples of this art online, using materials from coconuts, pumpkins, and watermelons (obvious candidates for carving) to daikon radishes and avocados. Get some inspiration from what you can find from some internet examples, then come up with your own creative ideas for how to turn food into art. The most advanced level of this kind of project would start with carving designs or objects into your ephemeral material – the food item itself – then transferring that to a wooden medium in order to preserve it. Either way, these kinds of creations have gained a lot of traction on the internet; you might find yourself followed by many for the wondrous creations you produce.

Painted Projects

If you have delved into more advanced projects, then you have certainly invested in some basic painting tools and activities that give your projects more flair and finish. Now you may want to invest a little more time learning a few more advanced painting techniques to make your projects stand out. Of course, the basics, as covered in the previous chapter, are still all very important: cleaning up your final project; sanding when and where is necessary; applying primer before painting; allowing your project to dry thoroughly in between each step; and finishing with some kind of seal will always be a part of the painting process. But there are a few additional techniques that can change the look of your project in various ways.

First, remember that preparing your surface is key; in fact, paint won't stick very well to sharp edges (even if it does for a moment, it will quickly be worn or chipped off). So, keep this in mind when deciding which projects to paint. Also, be sure that all surfaces are clean before you apply any primer or paint.

Second, when choosing primer, you have several options: water-based acrylic primer; oil-based primer; and pigmented shellac. These all have different applications. A water-based primer is good for most new woods, though avoid overly knotty or resinous surfaces, as it won't cover those as well. Water-based primers also dry quickly and can take two coats within just a few hours. Oil-based primers are appropriate when you plan to use oil paints, of course, and it penetrates more deeply than acrylic primers (especially good when you are using weathered, or found, wood). Pigmented shellac is used for woods that are exceptionally knotty or resinous; it can cling to those surfaces without bleeding through. It is also very fast-drying, allowing you to apply two coats within a couple of hours. It can be used underneath either water-based or oil-based paints.

WHITTLING

If you are tackling a big project, something that you want to last forever and have taken much time in creating, you might want to proceed with the additional step of checking your object for weak areas. Once the primer has dried overnight, sand again, then shine a bright light parallel to the surface, checking everywhere for shadows. If you see discolored, shadowy spots or other flaws, then you can re-sand and apply primer again, if you like. In extreme cases, you might want to apply a little putty to fill in a chip or gap before sanding and re-priming.

Once you are ready to paint, have all of your equipment ready to go, of course, and handle the brush with care. Target which areas you wish to paint and move quickly but carefully in applying the paint: you don't want the paint to start drying (it will start to form a kind of "skin," like you see on the top of some dairy products) as the paint will look uneven. Another tip is that it is better to apply two separate, thin coats of paint than to slather on one heavy coat; this often causes the paint to run or look uneven. If you are applying paint to larger objects, you might consider an additive such as Floetrol to your paint; this slows the drying time, helping paint strokes to level off. That way, you won't see the tell-tale signs of brush work in the finished product.

Finally, there are some other pro techniques that you can apply to change the look of the final product in unique ways. For example, you can create an aged patina by using various products, some as simple as vinegar and Vaseline, or you can use steel wool to scrape off areas of paint to show the wood beneath. You can also track down finishes that add a particular look to your project, such as aged copper, antiqued silver, whitewash, and faux marble tones. There are a wide variety of products available on the market now to produce that "distressed" or antique look. You can also apply various glazes which add to the shine of your finished product (or, alternately, tone down the brightness of a color, depending on what you want). Another widely available product is chalkboard paint, wherein you can turn just about any wooden surface into a chalkboard. One interesting idea with chalkboard paint is to create a faux menu board for your kitchen, so you can write the day's menu or grocery lists on a beautiful surface as if you were a café in Paris. This would also be a fun idea for childrens' rooms.

Make sure your paint is dry before moving to the next step, and always apply a seal for a lasting result. After sealing, you might also consider adding a finish or topcoat, especially if the object will be used regularly (instead of just displayed). These products include polyurethane spray, water-based polycrylic finish, and paste wax. Each of these have particular attributes that may just add the final touch to your carefully considered project.

WHITTLING

Survival Skills

Again, whittling is all about being situated in the great outdoors, so it is a perfect match for camping (remember the tent poles as in the previous chapter) and other outdoor activities. Sitting around a campfire and whittling random little projects from found wood is one of the great pleasures of the hobby. But you can also tackle some more ambitious projects out at your campsite, making useful items that can accompany you on your outdoor adventures.

For example, whittling a workable fishing spear isn't much different than carving out a tent stake. It's simply a larger project with a sharper end in its most basic form. But, with some slightly larger equipment (a machete or an ax), you can make a more sophisticated, pronged spear with a sturdy piece of wood. Use the machete to split the wood into four or more "prongs" coming up about a quarter of the length, then whittle each prong into a point. Tie some strong cord around the wood where the prongs meet the base for added strength and accuracy.

You can also make your own bow and arrow for a truly advanced project. Should you ever find yourself stranded out in nature, you can now arm yourself to take down some game, perhaps. Follow these instructions to try:

WHITTLING

- Find the right kind of wood for the project; in this case, you want a sturdy hardwood branch that is about six feet long and at least two inches in diameter. Try to find a branch that doesn't have any knots or protruding twigs, anything that you will have to work hard to remove or that may weaken the final product.

- Now test the wood to discover which way it naturally bends: press down on the upright branch, pushing gently into the ground, noting how the branch curves. The branch should naturally swivel in one direction, showing the way it inherently bends. Now you know which side is the "back" (outside of the curve) and which is the "belly" (inside of the curve). Try not to apply pressure to the back, as it can break.

- Mark the belly of the bow with a handhold about three inches out from the center in both directions. Above the handhold, the bow is called the upper limb; below the handhold is the lower limb.

- Now push down on the upright branch again, noting how the belly of the bow curves. Using careful strokes, whittle away the parts of the belly that are stiff, that don't bend with the natural curve. Remember: only carve on the

WHITTLING

belly side of the bow. You are trying to create one continuous and even curve.

- Then carve out notches on each tip of the bow (again, *only* on the belly side) for your string. Loop on your nylon or plant-based string at the notches, leaving about five or six inches of slack at the handhold (center) part of the bow. *Don't draw the bow yet*, or it can break.

- Now, hang the bow on a tree branch or other sturdy support so that it rests horizontally from the handhold. Then, pull on your string gently and steadily to check the evenness of the bow's curve, whittling away any uneven or stiff parts as you go; keep pulling gently but firmly to check for any stiff spots, whittling away when need be. This process is called "tillering," and it strengthens the bow. You want to continue to draw the string, correcting any problems with the belly's curve, until it is fully drawn – the length from the handhold to your jaw. You will know that the tillering is complete when both the upper limb and lower limb of the bow curve evenly as you draw fully.

- The bow can be used as is or you can take some time to finish it by sanding and sealing.

Some other useful items for outdoor adventures that you can work on is a walking stick, which can be just

WHITTLING

as simple as smoothing out a handle on a sturdy branch or as complicated as whittling a personalized design into the handle and/or shaft of the stick. If you do a lot of hiking, a customized walking stick might serve you well – and impress the rest of the pack. You can also quite easily make a slingshot out of a forked branch of found wood: simply debark the wood, measure out and carve your notches on each fork, then tie on your industrial-strength rubber band. Again, this can be easily personalized with designs, initials, and a little paint. This could keep you and your friends (or children) amused for hours, as long as you follow some basic safety standards so nobody gets hit in the eye. Finally, think of whittling away some standard utensils for use around the campfire: tongs for turning meat; forks for spearing items off the fire; or chopsticks for detail work.

hone your skills and produce a few small projects, you will start to find your inspiration for a collection or for a grander scheme.

You may find that you really enjoy carving animals and get better and better at making realistic versions of various animals: this turns into a menagerie of sorts or a traveling circus, or a diorama of a particular ecosystem with the flora and fauna to match. Or, you might find that you relish creating whimsical objects for the garden such as lawn gnomes and end up with a varied and unique collection that turns your lawn and/or garden into a fantasyland to delight the whole neighborhood. Or, you might find that you have a penchant for creating unique and durable children's toys, so you end up creating an entire line of items for various age groups. Or, you might find that you so enjoy the holiday projects that you create an entire elaborate display: say, a Santa's village, complete with elves, houses, snowmen, and reindeer; or a nativity scene complete with animals, magi, a manger, and so on; or, a spooky Halloween extravaganza with pumpkins, skeletons, bats, cats, witches and the like (or a Mexican "Day of the Dead" themed display). Or, you become fascinated by abstract designs and creative patterns, creating projects that are nothing more and nothing less than artful objects. Contrary to that, you might find yourself interested in creating practical, useful items for the kitchen or outdoor use. Or, you just might discover something

WHITTLING

Some Big Ideas

Finally, as has been mentioned throughout these last two chapters, consider your whittling work to be a fun hobby with potentially long-term payoffs; as you

WHITTLING

completely new and different, unique to your particular interests and skill set.

These considerations are not just purely academic, or random thought experiments; rather, they have the potential value of a hobby that turns into a lucrative side gig. With the advent of online crafts purveyors (Etsy being the most prominent), many people have found that their hobbies also appeal to others who will pay for the excellence of the handiwork and the uniqueness of the product. Of course, there is absolutely nothing wrong with enjoying whittling as a fun and simple hobby for your own personal pleasure, but if you start to invest a lot of time and energy into your work, you might find an audience who is ripe to receive it. Look to online sources for inspiration and education as to the kinds of projects that might catch on with a broader audience. You can also find a plethora of resources that will help you with whatever sorts of projects you become immersed in, from patterns and instructions to helpful step-by-step videos. Ultimately, the avid hobbyist will branch out on his or her own, creating their own original designs and objects, but you can gain knowledge and experience by following others at the beginning.

WHITTLING

In fact, there are many who believe that the fading art of whittling, other related woodworking, and other basic crafting skills expands our imagination and derives us of basic engineering knowledge that can lead to ingenious solutions to what look like intractable problems. It might be said that the junior whittler can become the senior engineer. These kinds of skills were once considered basic knowledge for all youngsters (at least all young men; although, that kind of gendered view has faded), and there is good reason to continue that tradition. We understand the world by interacting with it, and whittling is one of the ways in which we can continue to connect with nature in some form or fashion. It is not only that most whittling is practiced outdoors, perhaps around a campfire, it is also that we are using our native intelligence to create practical (and beautiful) objects out of wood, one of the most ubiquitous materials nature has to offer.

WHITTLING

WHITTLING

Chapter Summary

Embarking on some more advanced projects will further develop your whittling skills while giving you the opportunity to create gifts, unique decor, and even useful items for yourself, your family, and your friends.

- After you have mastered simple geometric shapes and abstract representations, you can move into more realistic and complex projects with greater level of detail.

- Think about your projects in a larger sense, about how each particular object can fit into a larger theme or creative expression.

- Your artistic creations can – and should – be shared with a wider audience.

WHITTLING

FINAL WORDS

Whittling is a time-honored tradition, a happy hobby for people who enjoy working with wood and, usually, being outside. It evokes images of wizened woodsmen shaving away at gnarled branches, sitting beside a campfire and drinking coffee out of a tin cup. And yet it encompasses so much more than the stereotypical image suggests: whittling isn't merely a way to while away the time; it is a folk tradition that, when practiced and perfected, can create beautiful objects and practical products. In short, whittling can be an outlet for expressions of creativity and artistry. It often leads to more advanced forms of woodworking, of course, but it is sufficient in and of itself to carve out fun and fascinating projects. Don't worry too terribly much about the difference between whittling and carving: while whittling, in its purest form, is the practice of carving an object from a single piece of wood using a simple knife, it is a basic form of carving. As you gain more skill and confidence, you will likely want to expand your basic whittling into some more complex woodworking; using hook knives and other specialty tools will give you an advantage should you wish to immerse yourself more fully into the hobby.

WHITTLING

For basic whittling, all you need besides an interest is a small knife and a piece of wood. Of course, there are other simple tools that can help you with more advanced projects, but one of the advantages of whittling as a hobby is that it is cheap and easy to get started. Advice on what kind of knife to get and how to keep it sharp is contained in the early part of this book, along with a discussion on the best kinds of wood you can use for various projects. A discussion of what kinds of wood are best for whittling can also be found, along with a primer on what kinds of basic cuts are frequently used in beginning whittling. Always remember, when whittling, to practice basic safety and to keep your knife well-sharpened.

The projects that you can undertake in your new-found hobby are nearly endless, from animals and wizards to toy trains and survival equipment. You can create holiday displays and whimsical home and garden décor, along with natural objects and personalized signs. As your skill set improves and your projects grow sturdier and lovelier, you can expand the quality of your finished products with paint and sealer, or more complex designs and unique flourishes. Once you become immersed in the hobby of whittling, you can begin to think of your creations as long-lasting one-of-a-kind objects to delight or to be used with care. Whittling becomes something that you can pass down to others, the skill itself or the objects you create, as well as a timeless pastime rooted in nature and folk art. Chances

WHITTLING

are you already have a pocket knife or the like: now just grab some wood and get started, whittling away the day!

www.ingramcontent.com/pod-product-compliance
Lightning Source LLC
Chambersburg PA
CBHW050323120526
44592CB00014B/2029